"Feeling jaded, weary, unsure that you can face Christmas this year?
This is a must read—perhaps as daily readings for December, but
once you start, it is so inspiring, provoking, relevant and unique that
you may want to read it all in one sitting."
—**Dr Peter Roennfeldt**, author, *Following Jesus*

"It is not easy to bring freshness to the story of Jesus' birth. Every year we relive the scenario; our children play their bit parts in the nativity play and the carols reverberate in our heads as we've walked through the crowded shopping malls. But Nathan Brown is a storyteller and, in his hands, this magnificent story comes to life. We enter the places, notice the presence of all the characters and feel the impact of the words as the gospels record it, as if for the first time. This is a beautiful collection. You will be drawn into the heart of incarnation—with all its earthiness, danger, inclusivity and glory."
—**Tim Costello**, AO, Director of Ethical Voice,
Executive Director of Micah Australia,
Senior Fellow of Centre for Public Christianity

"The Christmas story feels so familiar—the stable, the manger, the shepherds, the wise men—that meaning easily gets lost as we recite each part. *Advent* pulls together all the well known elements we love and invites us to refocus our attention back to the heart of Christmas to rediscover the beautiful richness of this age-old story."
—**Lyndelle Peterson**, pastor and national ministry leader

"At last, a re-telling of the story of Jesus' birth that peels away 2000 years of added Christmas schmaltz to focus on what was really happening. *Advent* unwraps God's gift of Jesus to reveal the depth and meaning of Jesus' birth for then and for now."
—**Dr Bruce Manners**, author, *The Command*

"*Advent* is like hearing a new bell sounding for Christmas. Nathan Brown has a way of pointing out the details and joining the dots to make the big picture meaningful again. Reconnecting with this peace and hope has never been more important."
—**Joanna Darby**, artist, teacher, author and activist

"I am genuinely excited to be adding *Advent* to my mix of Christmas traditions, to enjoy the rich depth that Nathan Brown brings with his insights into the story, the cultural context of the time and his own travels to the places in which this beautiful story unfolds. I know so many others will embrace this book as something they want to make a part of their journey in getting to know Jesus and the story of His birth."
—**Joshua Stothers**, pastor and podcaster, *Burn the Haystack*

Advent

Hearing the Good News in the Story of Jesus' Birth

NATHAN BROWN

SIGNS
PUBLISHING®
Established 1885

For more about this book, as well as the opportunity to purchase additional copies, visit **www.signspublishing.com.au/Advent**

Proudly published and printed in Australia by
Signs Publishing
Warburton, Victoria.

This book was
Edited by Lauren Webb
Proofread by Lachlan Garland
Cover and illustration design by Shane Winfield
Typeset in Berkeley Book 11.5/15.5

ISBN (print edition) 978 1 922373 22 9
ISBN (ebook edition) 978 1 922373 23 6

"Don't be afraid!" he said.
"I bring you good news that will bring
great joy to all people."

—Luke 2:10

To Angela

Contents

Invitation

It is easy to be cynical about Christmas. It is easy to be distracted by the cultural expectations and excesses of the season. It is easy to be busy with events and to-do lists, and to be stressed about the arrangements and dynamics of family gatherings. It is easy to think we have heard the story of Jesus' birth countless times before or to dismiss it as if it were merely another fairy story we tell to children.

I have experienced many of these things and have had more than a few "Bah, humbug" moments in responses to the familial, social, commercial and even religious expectations of a looming Christmas.

But, in my experience, something invariably happens as most of these pressures begin to subside. We arrive at the few days before Christmas and we slow our pace a little or, even amid these many other things, we take a few moments to get back to the story itself—and we begin to feel something of the wonder, humility, glory and good news of the story of the birth of Jesus. It might come with re-telling the story in some way, listening to or singing favourite Christmas carols, or whatever your family or faith traditions might be.

This book is an invitation to extend your focus on the story of Jesus' birth in this season. In the traditional Christian calendar, the four weeks leading up to Christmas were known as the season of Advent. It was a time to re-read and re-tell the stories surrounding His coming into the world and to reflect on different aspects and implications of this story.

Adapting that tradition, this book was written with 31 reflections that can be read daily throughout the month of December. Of course, you can choose to read it however you wish, but I invite you to see if taking regular time to reflect on this story might change your experience of this season. Or you might choose to make some other time to think about this remarkable story, which is no less true or important at any other time of the year.

If you have not previously spent much time with the story of Jesus and His birth, I invite you to spend this time considering the deeper significance and claims that surround this seemingly simple story. Despite all the cultural and historical additions and distractions, there must be reasons why so many people throughout history and even today have continued to re-tell and celebrate this story. I invite you to give it a hearing and an opportunity to catch your imagination.

If you know the story well, I invite you to re-hear the story, to think about it in some different ways or even to simply enjoy reflecting on it again. I have had the idea for this book for a number of years, which has prompted me to read and think about the story myself in some new ways. I have also had the privilege of visiting Bethlehem and some of the other places in the stories three times in the past few years and this has enhanced how I read and re-tell these stories. I hope I have brought the best of these reflections, study and experiences to this task of again telling the story of the birth of Jesus.

As a background to these reflections, I invite you to re-read the original stories of Jesus' birth: Matthew Chapters 1 and 2; Luke Chapters 1 and 2; and John Chapter 1. You will find these at the beginning of the New Testament in any edition of the Bible— although a contemporary translation of the Bible is easier reading— or you can find these freely online at various Bible websites.

To go deeper, pick one of the gospel stories of Jesus and read it through completely during this time. Luke's gospel is most referenced in these reflections, so reading through his account will give a fuller picture of Jesus' story and more insight into who He was, what He taught and what He did. I also encourage you to look up and read the verses around any of the Bible verses that are quoted or referenced if they catch your interest—there is always more to discover.

And once you have spent time with this book, I invite you to share it with someone else, whether in the form of the book itself or simply by sharing in a conversation about what you have learnt or appreciated. The best stories are worth re-telling, the best news is worth sharing.

As you read this book, I invite you to hear—or hear again—the good news in the story of Jesus' birth.

In the silence of a midwinter dusk there is far off in

the deeps of it somewhere a sound so faint that

for all you can tell it may be only the sound of the

silence itself. You hold your breath to listen. . . .

For a second you catch a whiff in the air of some

fragrance that reminds you of a place you have

never been and a time you have no words for.

You are aware of the beating of your heart.

The extraordinary thing that is about to happen

is matched only by the extraordinary moment

just before it happens.

Advent is the name of that moment.

—Frederick Buechner, "Advent," *Whistling in the Dark: A Doubter's Dictionary*, HarperSanFrancisco, 1993, page 3

1

(Good) News

Something happened.

Something significant happened—but in a way that seems so unlikely.

Yet something happened that was so significant that, every time we write the date, we remind each other that this thing happened a few more than 2000 years ago.

Something happened that was so significant that every year we pause and sing songs about it, share gifts with each other and re-tell the story.

Something happened in a particular place and time: in Bethlehem in the ancient land of Israel around the time of the empire-wide census decreed by Caesar Augustus—"the first census taken when Quirinius was governor of Syria" (Luke 2:2)—and nearing the end of the frenzied reign of Herod the Great, the Rome-supported king of the Jewish nation whose massive building projects were markedly more successful than his family relationships.

While the date of the Roman census is not clear historically, Herod's death is commonly dated to 4 BC and no later than 1 BC. The Bible records some key events as following the birth of Jesus: the arrival of the magi in Jerusalem, their search for Jesus in Bethlehem, the escape of Joseph, Mary and Jesus to Egypt, and Herod's massacre of all the children in Bethlehem under the age of two years old (see Matthew 2:1–18). If we factor in time for these events, it seems likely that Jesus was born between 6 and 4 BC. It might even have been a year or so earlier, with the news of Herod's death the all-clear signal allowing Joseph and Mary and their family to return from their refugee period in Egypt (see Matthew 2:19, 20).

So it seems that the monk who set the dates for the BC/AD divide might have been out by a few years. But in a remarkable twist of history, it was Jesus rather than Augustus, Quirinius or Herod—or any of the other powerful men and great leaders of their age—around whom the axis of history revolved. Something happened that truly changed the world.

The story is told in only two of Jesus' "official" biographies—the New Testament gospels. Matthew and Luke told the story of the birth of Jesus in ways that reflect their research interests and intended readerships. Matthew began with the Jewish genealogies and history, while Luke cited the Roman political leadership with its census and political administration. By contrast—in what is believed to be the first gospel to have been written—Mark seemed impatient to jump straight into the beginning of the ministry of Jesus. In the last of the gospels, John began with a poetic, philosophical and even cosmic meditation on light and darkness, Word and flesh, creation and life, but he still emphasised the historical reality of the One who became human and lived among humanity (see John 1:14), who had a particular history that had been experienced and witnessed.

Beyond the Bible, Jesus would become one of the most attested figures of ancient history. More is known of His life, His teachings and His death than is known about any of the powerful figures of that time, including those Luke used as markers: Augustus, Quirinius and Herod. Even if they debate some of the details and argue about their implications, no serious historian dismisses the reality of someone called Jesus of Nazareth, who lived in those places at that time. He was believed by many then and countless since to have been Someone significant—historically and spiritually. Something happened.

That such historical attention would be given to such an apparently inauspicious birth is notable. Of course, some of those who have come to be regarded among the great people of history were born

"I bring you good news that will bring great joy to all people."

in humble circumstances. Part of our interest in such stories of human achievement is how these people overcame their beginnings and aspired to the achievements for which they became known. Sometimes the date of their birth might come to be remembered and marked in retrospect, perhaps with a yearly festival in their city of birth. More often and quite understandably, their date of birth remains simply a historical fact and their later achievements receive more attention.

It is surprising that we know of Jesus' birth at all. A baby born to a poor, out-of-town couple in a small shepherd village in the Judean hills would not expect the fanfare accorded to children born in the homes of the powerful and wealthy. Given the limited record-keeping of the period, the time, place and circumstances of the birth of many people who would reach some kind of fame or notoriety is unknown. In one sense, the birth of Jesus might be considered one of those historical events that we look back on only after we see what He grew up to become.

But the story of Jesus' birth as told in the two gospels does not allow for that to be all there is to it. They assert that His birth was predicted, anticipated, announced, celebrated and noticed even in the halls of power and the courts of the temple. They urge that something significant happened in the fact of His birth in itself.

In Luke's telling of what happened that night in Bethlehem, there was an announcement of the birth of Jesus—only everything about it seemed unlikely, implausible and misdirected. An angel—a heavenly being sent as a messenger from God!—appeared to a group of shepherds, poor farm labourers employed to guard flocks of sheep overnight, to tell them that something had happened. And not just *something*, something big, something significant, something that would change the world, something that we might still be singing songs about and re-telling the story of more than 2000 years later: "I bring you *good news* that will bring great joy to all people" (Luke 2:10).

Something happened. Something real happened. Something significant happened. That's what makes it *news*.

Something overwhelmingly good happened. That's what makes it *good* news.

2

Anticipated

Many of us remember our anticipation of Christmas when we were children—and we can be reminded of this by observing our children or grandchildren, nephews and nieces today. Excitement builds through the various traditions that different families maintain. The marking of an Advent calendar, whether in a traditional format or a more commercial product, counts down the days to Christmas. At different dates and events, some kind of Christmas decorations or lights might be put up. Carols will begin to be sung—or heard on the instore music playlists and advertising jingles some weeks or even months earlier. Whether from a faith perspective or simply that of preparing for a family gathering with gifts and good food, the Christmas season fosters anticipation.

Apart from simply re-telling the story of Jesus' birth in the various ways that we do that, practising this sense of anticipation is perhaps one of the most authentic ways in which we mark the Christmas season. We can get a feel of this in the stories of Jesus' birth told by the gospel writers.

Matthew recited a brief history of the Jewish people, urging that these generations were all leading to this point in history. He also punctuated his storytelling with references and quotations from historical Hebrew prophecies about the birth of a coming Saviour. Luke told stories of startling angel appearances and unexpected pregnancies, with the sense that something was afoot that would have greater significance than the usual small-town birth. Of course, both gospels were written from a later vantage point, but even at the time of writing their stories retained a sense of expectation—as they do for us today.

But expectation was also in the spirit of the times that surrounded the birth of Jesus. For centuries after their return from exile in Babylon, the Jewish nation had been subjected to a series of conquerors and oppressors, with the Roman Empire the most recent and the most brutal. It had been about 400 years since the nation had received the prophecies of Malachi that close out the Bible's Old Testament. From this lapse in the Hebrew scriptures, it seems that most of those years had passed without authentic prophetic voices. But there were many pretenders who preyed on the people's hopes and fears. Historians report a succession of self-styled messiahs who had come and gone, often sparking violent uprising and even more violent repression. The people were looking for a leader who would set them free—but barely knew what this might mean.

Amid this cultural and political climate, there were those who continued to study their scriptures, to pray and to anticipate. They could answer the questions about a Messiah to come, a new king to be born. When the magi—or wise men—arrived in Jerusalem, Herod asked the religious leaders to direct their search. It seems they soon had the correct answer about where the Messiah was to be born from the Hebrew prophet Micah: "'In Bethlehem in Judea,' they said, 'for this is what the prophet wrote'" (Matthew 2:5).

When Jesus' cousin John began preaching, the questions from the religious leaders about who he was carried this same weight (see John 1:19–23). There was something in the air, an anticipation that could not help but foster hope, even after generations of silence, oppression and disappointment. And while there were more misunderstandings and disappointments to come, those who followed Jesus came to recognise that He was who and what they had been anticipating. Writing a few decades later, Paul, one of the students of those same religious leaders, would reflect on this anticipation: "But when the right time came, God sent his Son, born of a woman" (Galatians 4:4). In hindsight, it seemed to make sense to people like Paul.

"But when the right time came, God sent his Son, born of a woman."

But, despite the pervading sense of anticipation at the time of Jesus' birth, few were looking in the right places or anticipating in the right ways. An ageing priest and his barren wife were unlikely parents of one who would be a "voice shouting in the wilderness" (John 1:23) to proclaim the coming of the Messiah. A widow prophetess and an elderly scholar were the only ones who recognised something special about this eight-day-old baby when He was presented at the temple (see Luke 2:25–38). And coming from strange and foreign lands, the magi were curious heralds of the birth of a new Jewish king. But they each shared a holy sense of faithful anticipation.

To engage with the story of God and the central moment in which it specifically entered into human history in Jesus is to anticipate that God will act in our personal history and in the history of our world. That was the experience of those first few who recognised Jesus for who He was. They had a vibrant anticipation, a living hope based on the prophecies in the Hebrew scriptures of God's imminent intervention.

In Jesus, they recognised the reality of God's presence and action. Something was happening. The old man Simeon was content that his greatest hope in life had been fulfilled. "I have seen your salvation," he said, addressing his praise to God, "which you have prepared for all people. He is a light to reveal

God to the nations, and he is the glory of your people Israel!" (Luke 2:31, 32).

So when we return our attention each year to the story of the birth of Jesus, we practise anticipation. Even when crowded by Christmas events and the advertising and the shopping and the gifts and the cooking and all those other things on our holiday lists, we are reminded that this story has a momentum and a direction. A Baby was born—and in a sense it will be as if He is born again this year as we re-tell the story. When we see, even feel, the anticipation of our youngest and least jaded, we can see a small reflection of the anticipation expressed in the songs of Mary and Zechariah and the angels and the shepherds. We might also consider the patient faithfulness of Elizabeth and Anna, Simeon and the magi—and rediscover that the life of faith is seasoned with anticipation and hope.

3

Unexpected

Best known for his stories *The Hobbit* and *The Lord of the Rings*, J R R Tolkien was an Oxford scholar in linguistics, who made up languages for fun. He then wrote the histories of the people who spoke those invented languages. It just so happened that these became some of the best-loved stories in modern literature.

Reflecting on stories in an essay written in 1939,[1] Tolkien invented the term *eucatastrophe*. It describes the unexpected and seemingly unlikely turn of events in a story that produces a joyful ending and causes everyone to "live happily ever after" despite the threat, sorrow and evil that have gone before. A eucatastrophe is a "good catastrophe," something unexpected that happens to dramatically change the trajectory of the story.

As he considered the story at the heart of the Christian faith, Tolkien concluded that "the gospels contain a fairy story, or a story of a larger kind which embraces all the essence of fairy stories." What is remarkable is that the gospels—with elements and themes similar to the most compelling fairy story—are not fiction but history. The story of Jesus is "the greatest and most complete conceivable eucatastrophe," Tolkien wrote, before going on to emphasise, "But this story has entered History. . . . The Birth of Christ is the eucatastrophe of [human] history. The Resurrection is the eucatastrophe of the story of the Incarnation. The story begins and ends in joy."[2]

While an intervention from God was anticipated and hoped for by many people in the faith, culture and times in which Jesus was born, people were expecting the Messiah to be announced as a fully grown new king or national hero, preferably with military credentials and ambitions—not as a helpless baby. History does not usually pay attention to the newborn cries of a child of poor parents visiting a small village on the fringes of the empire.

Belying some traditions, we have little specific information about the magi—who they were, where they came from and why. But it seems they made the logical assumption in their search for "the newborn king of the Jews" (Matthew 2:2) and headed to Jerusalem and eventually to Herod's palace. Except for their inquiries, probably some months after Jesus' birth, this event would have gone unnoticed by the political and religious leaders in Jerusalem. Even then, it seems the disruption caused by these strange visitors was soon forgotten. To outside observers, there was nothing out of the ordinary in the birth of another boy in Bethlehem around the time of the census. And even if there was, Herod's murderous paranoia seemed to bring a quick and tragic end to that (see Matthew 2:16–18).

Of course, people do rise from obscure beginnings at different times in history. But their stories are told because they have overcome the anonymity of their birth and the tide of history that washed over them, threatening to sweep their memory away. The circumstances of Jesus' birth are not those that human understanding would choose or seek out if planning or expecting a shift in the power dynamics and structures of world history.

Jesus would be confronted by presumption and prejudice about his birth throughout the course of His life, which seemed to undermine any claims He might make about His mission and who He was. Not only was He seemingly conceived out of wedlock and born in an obscure town, but He grew up in the even smaller village of Nazareth in the hills of Galilee. "Can anything good come from Nazareth?" asked one of His earliest disciples (John 1:46). Even the hometown crowd in Nazareth rejected Him (see Luke 4:28–30). He had no formal education in the religious schools (see John 7:15), and He insisted on saying difficult and discomforting things, so "many

"For we were not making up clever stories when we told you about the powerful coming of our Lord Jesus Christ. We saw his majestic splendour with our own eyes."

of his disciples turned away and deserted him" (John 6:66). His rejection by the Jewish leaders and His grisly execution seemed the ultimate evidence of His failure and inevitable historical obscurity.

But the assertions contained in the stories of the birth of Jesus and the evidence of subsequent history are that something happened that night in Bethlehem that was profoundly significant in itself. This was a moment that marked a change in the course of history. To all but the most faithful—and even to them—this was a surprise: "Part of the meaning of the kingdom, in the four gospels, is precisely the fact that it bursts upon Jesus' first followers as something so shocking as to be incomprehensible."[3] It was counter-intuitive and unlikely. It was a good catastrophe but even then it was one that could easily be missed, at least in these early stages. But something had happened. The story of the birth of Jesus is a story of eucatastrophe.

So is it problematic to talk about the story of the birth of Jesus using the language of fairy stories? The temptation for those who choose to reject the stories and claims of Christianity as presented in the Bible would be to argue that the correlation with fairy stories is evidence of an element of fantasy or wishful thinking in Christian storytelling and belief. According to such an argument, the similarities between

Christianity and fairy stories might well be evidence of the fictional nature of the Christian story.

But such an allegation was anticipated—or at least responded to—by Jesus' first disciples: "For we were not making up clever stories when we told you about the powerful coming of our Lord Jesus Christ. We saw his majestic splendour with our own eyes" (2 Peter 1:16). While there are elements of the greatest human stories in the stories of Jesus' birth and His life, there is one significant difference: in Jesus, the fairy story became history—and that was the real and personal experience of the earliest followers of Jesus. Though they would not have used the term, they wrote a story of eucatastrophe because it was the story of what they had experienced. This was their story—and it was "too good not to be true."[4]

1. J R R Tolkien, "On Fairy-Stories" in *Tree and Leaf*, HarperCollins, 2001, page 72.

2. ibid.

3. N T Wright, *How God Became King: The Forgotten Story of the Gospels*, HarperCollins, 2012, page 197.

4. Frederick Buechner, *Telling the Truth*, HarperCollins, 1977, page 98.

4

Pre-existing

In the old town centre of Ulm, Germany, you might be walking along a seemingly ordinary cobblestoned commercial street and encounter a geometric brown-granite stone sculpture. It identifies the location of the house in which Albert Einstein was born on March 14, 1879. A few years ago, I was visiting friends in that historic town and we were enjoying a sunny autumnal afternoon exploring the city. Returning along the Bahnhofstrasse after visiting Ulm Minster—currently the tallest church building in the world—we came across this marker.

Such sites are curious places to visit—or stumble across, as in this instance. There were likely other children born in that house across the generations, but only young Albert is celebrated. There was nothing to see at the site besides the sculpture, since the actual house was destroyed by firebombing during World War II. And the location would have had little influence on Einstein's life as his family moved to Munich about a year after his birth. Yet we paused for a few minutes, read the inscriptions and felt the significance of this place for the story that had literally been birthed there.

Just as this spot in Ulm only gained significance after Einstein achieved fame, the place and story of a child's birth are usually only given significance retrospectively because of some future achievement. But in re-telling and memorialising the birth of Jesus, we are encountering something different. This is not an occasion to reflect on who this Baby would grow up to be, but on who He already was: "The solemnity and awe do not lie in the fact that the baby becomes the eternal Judge. What strikes us to the heart is this: the eternal Judge, very God of very God, Creator of the worlds, the Alpha and the Omega, has become that little baby."[1]

The summary of the Bible's New Testament is that something significant happened in the birth, life, death and resurrection of Jesus. This story was told from four different perspectives, and these gospels, as well as the history and letters that make up the bulk of the New Testament, represent the first and second generations of Jesus' followers working out what had just happened and what it meant for them, for their faith and for the world. Their conclusions and claims were startling.

The gospel of John is generally believed to be the last written in this collection of books, dated near the end of the first century. Rather than adding to the stories of the birth of Jesus and the unique circumstances in which that occurred, already told in the gospels of Matthew and Luke, the fourth gospel begins with some remarkable poetry. Echoing the Genesis-language of creation, we are introduced to an eternal and pre-existing Word:

> In the beginning the Word already existed.
> The Word was with God,
> and the Word was God.
> He existed in the beginning with God.
> God created everything through him,
> and nothing was created except through him.
> The Word gave life to everything that was created,
> and his life brought light to everyone (John 1:1–4).

A later convert and another of the New Testament writers, Paul, also employed similar cosmic imagery in trying to express the divine reality that the followers of Jesus realised in Him—something that was somehow a pre-existing and present reality in the birth of the Baby in Bethlehem:

> Christ is the visible image of the invisible God.
> He existed before anything was created and is supreme
> over all creation,

"Christ is the visible image of the invisible God. He existed before anything was created and is supreme over all creation."

for through him God created everything
in the heavenly realms and on earth.
He made the things we can see
and the things we can't see—
such as thrones, kingdoms, rulers and authorities
   in the unseen world.
Everything was created through him and for him.
He existed before anything else,
and he holds all creation together
(Colossians 1:15–17).

Of course, this was not immediately obvious to most of those who were in Bethlehem that night or even to many who encountered Jesus during the rest of His life. But among those who met Him—and particularly those who looked more carefully and listened longer—there were those who saw glimpses of the divine and who were undeniably transformed by such encounters. And as the community of believers continued to study and wrestle with who and what they had experienced, their understanding grew: "So the Word became human and made his home among us. He was full of unfailing love and faithfulness. And we have seen his glory, the glory of the Father's one and only Son" (John 1:14).

To whatever degree we consider this to be true, it is unsurprising that the place where Jesus was born in

Bethlehem—or which at least has been celebrated as His birthplace since the fourth century—is today a popular destination for pilgrimage. Naturally, the motivations for visits to the small grotto beneath the Church of the Nativity in Bethlehem are as varied as the countless people who have come from different faith traditions, cultures and nations around the world where His story has been told. But in the experience and understanding of those who were closest to the story, the birth of this Baby was the event in which human history intersected with God in a new and profound way. Something happened that changed God, that changed humanity and that changed history.

If we are tempted to think that the Christmas story is one of a poor but cute baby who grew up to be a great and good teacher—or some similarly reductionist re-telling of the story—we are soon confronted by a much larger set of questions and challenges. The claim that Jesus, the newborn baby of Bethlehem, was somehow God and the Creator of the world stretches us beyond science, history and all human knowledge. The claim is that something happened that is bigger than any story we might tell of it. As Lucy explained to the last king of Narnia in one of C S Lewis' much-loved stories, "In our world too, a Stable once had something inside it that was bigger than our whole world."[2]

Today, we might only have an approximate location of Jesus' birthplace, but this story should cause us to pause nonetheless and reflect on the baby born there. If we allow ourselves, we might begin to feel the wonder that left the shepherds "glorifying and praising God for all they had heard and seen" (Luke 2:20) and the writers of the rest of the New Testament grappling for words for the rest of the century.

---

1. Fleming Rutledge, *Advent: The Once & Future Coming of Jesus*, Eerdmans Publishing Co, 2018, page 60.

2. C S Lewis, *The Last Battle*, Fontana Lions, 1980, page 134.

5

Sent

How God works is one of the great mysteries of faith. But that He *does* work—in the history of our world and in each of our lives—is the primary reason we have faith at all. As much as we can know God, we know Him by what He has done.

One of our challenges in knowing and talking about God is language. Many of the ways in which we try to speak about or describe God are imprecise and inadequate. Even if we ask what God is *like*, we are suggesting that the best we might be able to offer by way of explanation are metaphors and approximations. This is why the stories of God matter. In the story of the birth of Jesus, we can see God at work and learn something more of how God acts.

This specific story began with an angel appearing to Mary in the village of Nazareth. It is commonly believed that she was a teenager at the time, engaged to be married to an older craftsman in the village. When told she was going to have a baby, Mary asked how this would be possible. The angel's response gives an insight into the nature of God and how God works. The angel replied to Mary: "The Holy Spirit will come upon you, and the power of the Most High will overshadow you. So the baby to be born will be holy, and he will be called the Son of God" (Luke 1:35).

In this apparently simple statement, we hear the announcement of something remarkable that was about to happen—and we are introduced to a God who is a loving community of three Persons who act together as One in intent, intellect and integrity. In turn, we are introduced to the Holy Spirit, the Most High—or God the

Father—and God the Son, who would become human as Jesus while remaining essentially God.

The theological term for this community of three Persons is *Trinity* and it is one of the most complex concepts of Christian faith, knotted up with the intricacies and inadequacies of language, metaphor and our limited human capacity for understanding the transcendent and Divine. Yet it makes most sense in a story like this, as well as other glimpses we see throughout the life and teachings of Jesus: "If the story of what happens with Jesus could be told without a threefold reference to God there would be no church doctrine of the Trinity."[1]

In the Bible's larger story, the three-in-one God worked together to create the world as a shared project of love, inviting the first human beings into their loving and equitable community. When that God–human relationship was broken, God had a plan for overcoming the sin and death that had been brought into the world, with each of the Persons of God playing distinct but equally engaged roles in the project of reclaiming and restoring humanity, our broken relationships and all of creation.

This is the context of the Bible's best-known verse—and the lesser-known but equally important verse that follows it: "For God loved the world so much that he *gave* his one and only Son, so that everyone who believes in him will not perish but have eternal life. God *sent* his Son into the world not to judge the world, but to save the world through him" (John 3:16, 17).[2] We will come back to talking more about the love of this God who would reach out to a broken world. But, for the moment, we simply observe the action of God as He *gave* and *sent* a unique part of His triune Self into our world as a baby born in Bethlehem at the specific time in history when Augustus and Herod ruled the world.

While exactly how God works remains a mystery, this story shows us God in action. Because Luke was explicit in recognising the presence and actions of the trinity of God in his telling of the story, we can begin to understand this oft-heard story with new depth and step further into the mystery of the nature of God. This is also

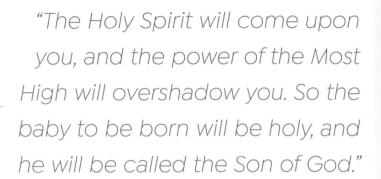

"The Holy Spirit will come upon you, and the power of the Most High will overshadow you. So the baby to be born will be holy, and he will be called the Son of God."

an invitation to appreciate more of God's world-creating and world-changing love. We not only see a baby, but a Baby who was sent as a divine emissary; He was not merely an agent of God, but truly the Son of God.

As they had at the conception of His life, these three Persons would appear together at Jesus' baptism, which marked the beginning of His public ministry about 30 years later:

> One day when the crowds were being baptised,
> Jesus himself was baptised. As he was praying,
> the heavens opened, and the Holy Spirit, in bodily
> form, descended on him like a dove. And a voice
> from heaven said, "You are my dearly loved Son,
> and you bring me great joy" (Luke 3:21, 22).

As at his conception, at Jesus' baptism we again observe the community, love and joy that are the reality and essence of what God is. The Trinity was seen together as Jesus was anointed and sent to serve the world in His life and ministry and to save and restore it by His death and resurrection. This is why, for all its complexity, metaphor and abstraction, "the doctrine of the Trinity is ultimately a practical doctrine with radical consequences for Christian life."[3] We see what God is like and how God works by what God does. Not only that, but we are invited to join with God in what He is doing in our world.

And when we re-tell the story of the birth of Jesus, we are drawn into the wonderful mystery of God and His work in our world. We are awed by how something so significant and grand could be made so specific and small. And we are overwhelmed by the depth of love within this intimate creative community that compelled it to send One of their Three-in-One into a broken and dangerous world, risking rejection and defeat, to offer the invitation to reconciliation, restoration and re-creation.

1. Christopher Morse, *Not Every Spirit: A Dogmatics of Christian Disbelief* (2nd edition), Continuum, 2009, page 128.

2. New Living Translation footnote, alternative translation, my emphasis.

3. Catherine Mowry LaCugna, *God For Us: The Trinity and Christian Life*, HarperOne, 1991, page 1.

6

Incarnation

There are so many reasons Christmas should have lost its significance:

> The lovely old carols played and replayed till their effect is like a dentist's drill or a jack hammer, the bathetic banalities of the pulpit and the chilling commercialism of almost everything else, people spending money they can't afford on presents you neither need nor want. "Rudolph the Red-Nosed Reindeer," the plastic tree, the cornball crèche, the Hallmark Virgin. Yet for all our efforts, we've never quite managed to ruin it. That in itself is part of the miracle.[1]

Despite its many distractions and diversions—and we could each add to this list from our own experiences and holiday aggravations—that Christmas continues to have some meaning is testimony to the grand miracle at its core. That miracle can be summed up in a single word: incarnation. God became human. More than that, God became a fragile and helpless baby. The Creator came to His creation, the One who made it all dependent on others for His most basic needs. It is a miracle and mystery always beyond our understanding.

If we get to it among the busyness of the season, each year we are invited again to imagine what the "first Christmas" must have been like. Growing up in a church context, I have many memories of watching—and sometimes participating in—re-creations of nativity stories. These often featured a group of children dressed in an assortment of towels, bed sheets, bath robes and dressing gowns in a cardboard stable with bales of hay strewn across the front of the church or school hall. While the production values of some church nativity plays seem to have improved, many nativity stories and scenes retain their comic amateur earnestness. Even some grandparents will admit that these can sometimes be difficult to sit through and often hardly seem appropriate re-creations of a story which has such profound claims made about it.

Yet somehow—perhaps almost incidentally—they can begin to work, if we allow ourselves to be drawn into the story. In the frailty of the expression, with all its human sincerity and frantic indifference, we might experience and gain an insight into something of the feebleness of this eternal and central moment.

Only in our re-tellings does the world stop for this event. As a starting point, the shepherds were simply going about their work. We have hints that the village of Bethlehem was crowded: "there was no lodging available for them" (Luke 2:7). Many of the local residents and businesses were probably busy housing and feeding the influx of visitors, while the out-of-towners were intent on either rest or revelry, perhaps excitedly catching up with distant relatives or letting off steam after a journey they had been forced to make by their Roman occupiers. It was probably not a silent night and any attending holiness would have been largely unappreciated. Only a small number of people in town that night even knew of Jesus' birth; fewer still had any clue as to its significance.

Only in retrospect could John say, "we have seen his glory" (John 1:14). But in that long-ago animal shelter, the largely ignored birth was already a new and glorious reality: "So the Word became human and made his home among us. He was full of unfailing love and faithfulness" (John 1:14).

But there is a darker reality to the story of the birth of Jesus. While the angels sang glory to God for this marvellous thing that had happened (see Luke 2:13, 14), it seems they might have been just as likely to hold their collective breath in fearful wonder and with a

"So the Word became human and made his home among us. He was full of unfailing love and faithfulness."

sense of foreboding at the vulnerability into which this Child had been birthed. In Jesus, God was entering into the risks of this world. The life and experience of Jesus would include all our human and physical dangers, with more than the usual risk of political, physical and spiritual attacks. He would be a target, as would those who cared for Him and followed Him. Only the eternal reward is greater than this incalculable risk.

Incarnation, as Frederick Buechner has described it, "is not tame. It is not touching. It is not beautiful. It is uninhabitable terror. It is unthinkable darkness riven with unbearable light."[2] Perhaps one of the reasons that our various depictions, re-creations and re-enactments of the nativity story seem inadequate is that, for all their earnestness, we don't take the story seriously enough. Incarnation is dangerous.

In the sentimentality of Christmas stories re-told, we must not forget that His human birth made it possible for God to die. He faced life-threatening danger almost immediately. In Matthew's telling of the story, Joseph, Mary and Jesus were forced to run from the paranoid and murderous King Herod soon after the visit of the magi (see Matthew 2:13–15). But incredibly, in the Bible's narration of Jesus, it seems that the eventual death of this miracle Baby was one of the key purposes of His birth.

We can marvel at the sacrifice of God stooping so low as to

become human. Yet He would go lower still. The darkness of His crucifixion 30-something years later and the light of the resurrection morning a couple of days after that are the source of our true hope. This light flickered weakly in the first cries of the baby-God but would come to shine far brighter than the lantern light in a stable or even the angel glow depicted on Christmas cards: "The Word gave life to everything that was created, and his life brought light to everyone" (John 1:4).

From that night, a powerful light has been shining in the darkness of ourselves, our world, our despair and hopelessness. But it is sad to say that "the darkness has not understood it" (John 1:5, footnote). The tackiness, artificiality and stylised good will of our contemporary Christmases so clearly show that we have not understood it still. Yet that Light continues to shine its piercing beam into our darkness. God became light in the hope of being understood by the darkness. It is the central miracle of incarnation.

1. Frederick Buechner, *Whistling in the Dark: A Doubter's Dictionary,* HarperSanFrancisco, 1993, page 29.

2. ibid, page 30.

7

Fear

Despite the risks inherent in incarnation, there is a significant and repeated pattern in the succession of announcements that preceded and accompanied the birth of Jesus.

While the elderly priest Zechariah was fulfilling his duties in the temple, burning incense as part of the ritual of afternoon prayers, an angel appeared to him, introducing himself as Gabriel, a messenger who had come directly from the presence of God. "Zechariah was shaken and overwhelmed with fear when he saw him. But the angel said, 'Don't be afraid, Zechariah! God has heard your prayer'" (Luke 1:12, 13).

We don't know the specific circumstances in which this same angel also appeared to Mary, but the tradition marked by the Basilica of the Annunciation—a relatively contemporary and beautiful church in Nazareth today, built over the archaeological site of a small ancient house—suggests that Mary would have been going about the daily domestic duties of a young woman of her time. Gabriel addressed Mary with a strange greeting from God, leaving her "confused and disturbed." But he was quick to add, "Don't be afraid, Mary" (Luke 1:29, 30).

When Joseph learned of his betrothed Mary's sudden and inexplicable pregnancy, he was understandably and righteously troubled and decided that he could not go ahead with their marriage. But an angel appeared to him in a dream to reassure him. "'Joseph, son of David,' the angel said, 'do not be afraid to take Mary as your wife'" (Matthew 1:20).

On the night Jesus was born, shepherds were guarding their sheep in the fields outside the village of Bethlehem. We might imagine a small group of men sitting and talking quietly together, perhaps complaining about the influx of census-compelled visitors. The night would be dark, lit only by moon and stars, perhaps a small fire for some light and warmth.

> Suddenly, an angel of the Lord appeared among them,
> and the radiance of the Lord's glory surrounded them.
> They were terrified, but the angel reassured them. "Don't
> be afraid!" he said. "I bring you good news that will
> bring great joy to all people" (Luke 2:9, 10).

One of the repeated refrains of the story of the birth of Jesus is "Don't be afraid." It is hardly surprising. "Don't be afraid" is most often an acknowledgment that there is a likelihood of fear. In each of these instances, the immediate circumstances are the most obvious reason for fear. The heavenly messenger, the unexpected pregnancy, the sudden interruption were alarming. "Don't be afraid" was an important and necessary introduction.

But there seems to be a larger meaning in these comforting commands. As we have considered, the incarnation was not a project for the faint-hearted:

> Terror surrounded the life of Jesus like great parentheses.
> At His birth, Herod pursued Him with slaughter, and in
> His crucifixion, He shared the fate of the condemned
> slaves and others of low esteem. But Jesus was not
> contained by the terror, for at His birth and at His
> resurrection, messengers from God proclaimed for all
> who would hear: "Do not be afraid."[1]

But there is a still larger understanding of the angels' words. "Do not be afraid" is one of the Bible's most common commands. Of course, it is a common greeting when an angel appears or God shows up in some kind of dramatic or unexpected way. But, much more than this, it is one of the key messages of the Bible.

"Do not be afraid" acknowledges the real human experience of

"But the angel said, 'Don't be afraid, Zechariah! God has heard your prayer.'"

fear, the tangible and sometimes intangible nature of the threats that surround us in the world as we know it, and our frailty as human creatures. It recognises the existential crisis of death and how it works to undermine all that is good, worthwhile and true about our lives. It also reflects the broken relationships with which we live, which can threaten our peace, security and even our lives.

"Do not be afraid" also reflects our broken relationship with God. In the Bible's story of the human fall away from God, Adam's first confession is that fear had replaced the community they had previously experienced with God: "I heard you walking in the garden, so I hid. I was afraid because I was naked" (Genesis 3:10). This fear was the first barrier God would need to overcome in restoring our relationship with Him. But at the same time, the evil at work in our world would continually work to entrench and grow the human fear of God.

With this background, it is hardly surprising that "Do not be afraid" would become one of the recurring themes in the life and teaching of Jesus. It was a necessary reassurance when the disciples were exposed to glimpses of Jesus' divinity (see Matthew 17:1–8) and a catalyst for their choice to follow Him (see Luke 5:8–11). In Jesus teaching, it was also a practical and spiritual ingredient for living life with God: "So don't be afraid, little flock. For it gives your Father great happiness to give you the Kingdom" (Luke 12:32).

So the "Do not be afraids" in the stories surrounding the birth of Jesus were laden with meaning, both practical and deeply spiritual. They introduced the people in the stories to the divine and recognised their humanity. They announced that God was about to do something new in the history of our world, which would be troubling, transformative and redemptive.

It was almost a year after his startling conversation with the angel in the temple that Zechariah, old priest and delighted new father, could speak again. No longer fearful but "filled with the Holy Spirit," he used his first words well in a bold song of prophecy and praise for what God was doing in the world:

> Praise the Lord, the God of Israel, because he has visited and redeemed his people. . . . We have been rescued from our enemies so we can serve God without fear, in holiness and righteousness for as long as we live. . . . Because of God's tender mercy, the morning light from heaven is about to break upon us, to give light to those who sit in darkness and in the shadow of death, and to guide us to the path of peace (Luke 1:68–79).

And "awe fell upon the whole neighbourhood, and the news of what had happened spread throughout the Judean hills" (Luke 1:65).

1. Lee Griffith, *The War on Terrorism and the Terror of God*, Eerdmans Publishing, 2002, page 278.

8

Human

In Luke's gospel, Jesus was introduced to His mother Mary by the angel Gabriel in this way: "You will conceive and give birth to a son, and you will name him Jesus. He will be very great and will be called the Son of the Most High" (Luke 1:31, 32). A few verses later, Gabriel re-affirmed, "he will be called the Son of God" (Luke 1:35). Later, God Himself confirmed this remarkable, specific and unique claim about Jesus. At His baptism a "voice from heaven said, 'You are my dearly loved Son'" (Luke 3:22); at His transfiguration, the voice again announced, "This is my Son" (Luke 9:35).

Curiously, elsewhere in the gospels this "Son of God" title is used almost exclusively by Jesus' enemies. Evil spirits recognised Him by this title, the devil in his temptations of Jesus tried to make Him doubt that the title was His, and religious and political leaders used it as the basis for accusing Jesus of blasphemy or mocking Him during His trial and crucifixion. In the mouths of His enemies, tempters, critics and persecutors, "Son of God" became a term of derision and irony, a joke commenting on His seemingly ordinary and ultimately tragic circumstances.

By contrast, Jesus' favourite description of Himself was the less obvious and seemingly contradictory expression "Son of Man." It is used about 80 times through the four gospels but only ever by Jesus—and only ever about Himself. Those who first heard these statements would have understood the title as a reference to the expression used in the book of Daniel (see Daniel 7:13). But it also suggests that while Jesus understood that He was God, He was focused on identifying as human, rather than starting out as a human who aspired to be identified as God.

We are given a snapshot of His recognition of God as His Father from as early as the age of 12 (see Luke 2:49), so the process by which He developed His understanding of His unique divine–human identity likely began with stories Mary told Him about the circumstances of His birth. But the process of working out His identity as a young person might have been progressive as part of His maturation—as He "grew in wisdom and in stature and in favour with God and all the people" (Luke 2:52). With this growing realisation, Jesus' preference for the expression "Son of Man" might suggest that it was more surprising to Him that He was human than that He was God.

Likely responding to some of the first-century critics and those who wanted to overly spiritualise the story of His life, the gospel writers were specific in depicting Jesus as human. At times, amid His teaching, miracle-working and healing, Jesus was portrayed as tired, hungry, thirsty, angry and nearly overwhelmed with grief and despair. He famously wept at the tomb of a friend (see John 11:35) and endured the pain and humiliation of His crucifixion. We can also find moments of joy, excitement, celebration and humour—although these are sometimes less obvious in the way we usually read these ancient and foreign stories.

In the gospels, Jesus was undeniably human—and through the experiences of Jesus, God knows directly what the human experience feels like. Stepping into our world, with all its joys and challenges, He has become literally, physically and emotionally one of us. Because of Jesus, we can no longer accuse God of being remote, unfeeling or uncaring. One of the names given to Jesus in Hebrew prophecy summarised this aspect of who Jesus was: "She will give birth to a son, and they will call him Immanuel, which means 'God is with us'" (Matthew 1:23). Drawing on a similar theme, John described how God-in-Jesus "made his home among us" (John 1:14).

But this identification went further. This wasn't just a nice idea

"She will give birth to a son, and they will call him Immanuel, which means 'God is with us.'"

or a pleasant Christmas sentiment. In the society and political culture in which we live, it is remarkable—and it should be jarring—to realise the extent to which Jesus identified with so much of human experience, particularly the experience of those on the margins of our societies. He was a refugee and asylum seeker, a homeless guy, a target of religious intolerance, a member of an oppressed people group, a victim of torture and monstrous injustice, even someone who doubted the presence and goodness of God (see Matthew 27:46). The story of Jesus finds echoes in the worst and most challenging human experiences of both history and headlines. As "Son of Man," Jesus identified with us in so many ways—many of them surprising and difficult.

This identification with human suffering was so significant and locked in to such a degree that Jesus would teach that to help those in need or otherwise hurting was to help and serve Him. In a story He told, figuratively depicting the final judgment of humanity, He made this point clear:

> Then the King will say to those on his right, "Come, you who are blessed by my Father, inherit the Kingdom prepared for you from the creation of the world. For I was hungry, and you fed me. I was thirsty, and you gave me a drink. I was a stranger, and you invited me into your home. I

was naked, and you gave me clothing. I was sick, and you cared for me. I was in prison, and you visited me."

. . . And the King will say, "I tell you the truth, when you did it to one of the least of these my brothers and sisters, you were doing it to me!" (Matthew 25:34–36, 40).

By becoming human while remaining God, Jesus transformed humanity, redefining what it means to be human and even recalibrating the relationships between each of us. The miracle of Jesus' incarnation as the "Son of Man" calls us to love others, even amid the headlines, politics and injustices of our time and place: "For even the Son of Man came not to be served but to serve others and to give his life as a ransom for many" (Matthew 20:28).

9

Conflict

Some years ago, I had the opportunity to work closely with a friend and colleague who is a storyteller. Not only would he entertain us with amusing anecdotes around the office, but Dave has also travelled around the world to tell stories. His specialty is creatively re-telling Bible stories—usually specifically for children, but more often enjoyed by everyone listening.

So it came as a particular challenge to him when one of his then school-aged sons one evening said that he didn't want to hear another one of those "boring" Bible stories from Dave. This caught his attention and he asked what kind of story he would like to hear instead. His son explained that he wanted to hear a story with dragons and swords and all that kind of adventure.

Dave thought about this for a little while, accepted the challenge and came up with a new story to add to his repertoire. It was a story of a fearsome and strange red dragon—"seven heads and 10 horns" kind of strange—who with the swinging of its tail swept one-third of the stars from the sky. But there was an unusual focus to the dragon's anger. There was a woman who was about to give birth to a baby—a Baby who would grow up to rule all the nations. But when her son was born, both the child and the woman had to be rescued from the dragon and its murderous anger.

In a series of breathtaking escapes, the woman miraculously sprouted wings to evade the dragon, who then unleashed a magic-but-menacing flood to engulf and drown her. But she was rescued again, this time by the earth itself, which swallowed the flooding water. Foiled in this plot but still enraged, the dragon continued to hunt the woman and fight against the kingdom that rightfully belonged to the child.

Not only did Dave tell this story to his children, but I heard him tell it at large churches and conferences too. This story grew into a book, then a series of books, sharing stories and themes from the Bible in some new and creative ways.[1]

It's a dramatically different way of telling the story of the birth of Jesus—not the usual Christmas card imagery of nativity scenes but imagery that highlights the remarkable cosmic significance of His birth. It was a story first told in such a manner in the book of Revelation, a seemingly fantasy-themed vision that depicts a universe-sized conflict, including a war between God and his angels against the dragon—who is named as Satan—and the angels who followed him in rebellion against God. After being beaten back and pushed out of heaven, the focus of the rebellion and action of this story shifted to this planet, where the dragon continued to roam and rage.

And where a Baby was to be born.

Again it seemed an improbable victory, an unexpected twist in the story, an unlikely Hero. However, in the midst of Revelation 12, a loud voice proclaims the significance of this seemingly fantastic vision: "It has come at last—salvation and power and the Kingdom of our God, and the authority of his Christ" (Revelation 12:10).

The reality of a cosmic conflict is one that recurs from time to time throughout the Bible, but it is made most explicit in Revelation 12's vivid imagery and re-telling of the story of the coming of Jesus. And one of the intriguing and revelatory insights is that this is an ongoing war—the woman and her other children are ongoing targets of the dragon's anger.

There are further hints of this background war that appear in Jesus' story. While still an infant, an attempt was made on His life, and He and His family escaped through the night to the safety of Egypt as Herod's soldiers murdered the baby boys of Bethlehem

"It has come at last—salvation and power and the Kingdom of our God, and the authority of his Christ."

(see Matthew 2:13–18). He was directly tempted by the devil, whose attacks specifically included competing claims over who this world's kingdoms should belong to and who should be worshipped (see Matthew 4:1–11). Jesus regularly confronted evil spirits who claimed the right to dominate and possess people's lives—and He rebuked the evil spirits and sent them away. He taught His followers about the choice between good and evil and urged a kind of religion that set people free. And later New Testament writers would describe how, by His death and resurrection, Jesus confronted and comprehensively defeated the powers of evil, sin and death (see, for example, 1 Corinthians 15).

C S Lewis was a scholar who was alert to this kind of storytelling. In fact, he credited his friend, storyteller and author J R R Tolkien, with his own conversion to faith in the God and stories of the Bible. Lewis commented on his discovery of these story elements in the Bible:

> One of the things that surprised me when I
> first read the New Testament seriously was that
> it talked so much about a Dark Power in the
> universe—a mighty evil spirit who was held to be
> the Power behind death and disease, and sin. . . .
> Christianity thinks this Dark Power was created
> by God, and was good when he was created, and

went wrong. Christianity agrees with Dualism that this universe is at war. But it does not think this is a war between independent powers. It thinks it is a civil war, a rebellion, and that we are living in a part of the universe occupied by the rebel. . . . Christianity is the story of how the rightful king has landed, you might say landed in disguise, and is calling us all to take part in a great campaign of sabotage.[2]

It is not the way we usually tell the story of Jesus' birth, but it is an important way of understanding more of what it was about, the scale of what happened in the birth of Jesus and why it matters.

1. See David Edgren, *The Serpent Scroll*, Pacific Press Publishing Association, 2009.

2. C S Lewis, *Mere Christianity*, Fount Paperbacks, 1981, page 45.

10

Kingdom

One of the things we can miss in reading the stories of the Bible is a sense of the millennia that separate the history of the people it records. So let's try a little perspective. As a starting point, at the time of Jesus, the stories of Abraham—commonly accepted as the ancestor of the world's three major monotheistic faiths—were almost as long ago as the stories of Jesus or the various Caesars of Rome are to us today. The stories of Moses, the great liberator of the people of Israel, were as old as the stories of King Arthur and the Knights of the Round Table or the Prophet Muhammad and the beginnings of Islam are to us. We know of these stories but they seem incredibly old.

The reigns of David and his son Solomon as kings of Israel were closer to the time of Jesus and his contemporaries. Yet even these kings—who held a significant place in the national consciousness and imagination of the Jewish people—are dated to about 1000 years before the time of Jesus. For context, we are talking about a similar time gap from us back to historical figures such as William the Conqueror, Genghis Khan and Marco Polo. While these are names we might know, they are distant figures and, unless we have specifically studied their life and times, we tend to know little about them, even with all our easy access to information and historical documents. Contrast this with the semi-literate societies of ancient Judea, in which "publishing" was expensive and laborious, so most history was transmitted by oral storytelling.

Despite their age, the stories of the reign of the House of David were loved dearly by first-century Jews and the time was considered to be the golden age of their nation. These kings brought together the tribes of Israel into a more unified nation. David was a military hero, who defeated many of their national enemies, established Jerusalem as their capital city and expanded the nation's borders to their greatest extent. Capitalising on the ensuing time of comparative peace, Solomon made alliances with surrounding nations as trading partners, growing the nation's economic wealth and undertaking major building projects. One of these was the temple in Jerusalem— the central focus for their religion, politics and identity. Even today, many conservative Israelis look back to these stories as the golden age of their nation and a blueprint for the place they believe Israel should have in the world.

Until the past few decades, little has been known about these kings outside the Bible's histories. A succession of recent archaeological discoveries has added significantly to our knowledge of their times and the veracity of aspects of the Bible's historical record. But even though archaeology is confirming the Bible's account of these people for us, it is clear that the people of Jesus' time knew about these kings and kingdoms. They were very real to them. And in the context of their national history, the words "king" and "kingdom" pointed to something so much better than their occupation by the Roman armies and all the evil and oppression that entailed. It is not accidental that such language found its way into the story of Jesus and became a recurring way of talking about His identity and mission.

Both Matthew and Luke make it clear right at the beginning that the family into which Jesus was born was descended from the line of King David (see Matthew 1:6, Luke 1:27). This family history was the reason the family travelled to Bethlehem for the census and was there at the time Jesus was born: "Because Joseph was a descendant of King David, he had to go to Bethlehem in Judea, David's ancient home. He travelled there from the village of Nazareth in Galilee" (Luke 2:4)—more than a week's journey, either by foot or donkey. It

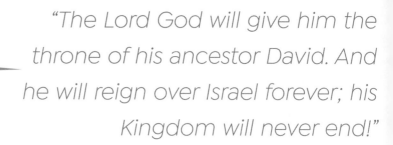

"The Lord God will give him the throne of his ancestor David. And he will reign over Israel forever; his Kingdom will never end!"

might seem a historical coincidence, but Jesus was linked to the stories of Israel's great and ancient kings even by geography.

The angel who announced the birth of Jesus to Mary some months earlier in Nazareth made this link much more explicit. It wasn't accidental or incidental. Speaking of the Baby that Mary would have, the angel made this bold claim: "The Lord God will give him the throne of his ancestor David. And he will reign over Israel forever; his Kingdom will never end!" (Luke 1:32, 33).

Religiously and politically, this was startling and audacious. Particularly so, when describing an unborn child. Yet the Hebrew scriptures had promised a ruler who would fit this description, something Zechariah celebrated in his song at the birth of John: "Praise the Lord, the God of Israel, because he has visited and redeemed his people. He has sent us a mighty Saviour from the royal line of his servant David, just as he promised through his holy prophets long ago" (Luke 1:68–70). He recognised that God was at work.

But this was also dangerous. To proclaim or even suggest the birth of a new king got people killed. The paranoid Herod had already killed a number of his family members for fear that they might try to take his place, so the magi's questions about a new king were troubling, not only to Herod but to "everyone in Jerusalem" (Matthew 2:3). Matthew recorded, "About that time some wise men from eastern lands arrived in Jerusalem, asking, 'Where is the newborn king of the Jews? We saw his star as it rose, and we have come to worship him'" (Matthew 2:1, 2). We don't know how or why they came to be looking for a king, but the references to kings elsewhere in the story show that they were right, and Herod's response in pre-emptively killing the baby boys of Bethlehem (see Matthew 2:16, 17) shows why it mattered.

Living in modern nations—even if still nominally governed by a monarchy—many of us do not fully understand the significance of a king and his kingdom, at best a mutually beneficial and necessary relationship between a leader and his people. Of course, it is also a power structure that has often been abused throughout history. But it is one of the ways in which the Bible story explains who Jesus was and what He did. The "kingdom of heaven" was to become the most common theme in Jesus' teaching, established in and by Jesus as an alternative to the political, economic and religious powers that dominated the world of those who heard and followed Him.

Standing trial before the Roman governor of Judea at the end of His life, Jesus affirmed this different but no less real kingdom: "My Kingdom is not an earthly kingdom" (John 18:36). The outcome of His trial proved His point but also demonstrated the political reality of His claim. As the angel had at the announcement of His impending birth, the charge sheet posted above His crucifixion proclaimed, "Jesus of Nazareth, the King of the Jews" (John 19:19).

This was not the golden age of a new kingdom that many would have imagined or hoped for when the story of Jesus' birth began. But somehow, tragic and horrific as it was, it was also the beginning of a new and more enduring kind of kingdom—and a story that humanity continues to re-tell thousands of years later.

11

Revolution

When the angel Gabriel appeared to Mary, he announced that she was "favoured" by God and He was with her. So it might seem strange to us that God's presence in her life would look like an unconventional and unexplainable pregnancy that would risk her prospective marriage, her place in her community and potentially even her life. But Gabriel concluded with the assurance that she would not be alone in this unique predicament. The angel directed her to someone who would understand: "What's more, your relative Elizabeth has become pregnant in her old age! People used to say she was barren, but she has conceived a son and is now in her sixth month. For the word of God will never fail" (Luke 1:36, 37).

Only a few days later—before she would have to face the awkward questions of her fiancé and family, as well as the gossip and accusations of the people of her village—Mary "hurried to the hill country of Judea [the region around Bethlehem] to the town where Zechariah lived. She entered the house and greeted Elizabeth" (Luke 1:39, 40). While the details provided in the story are limited, the portrayal of the meeting between Mary and Elizabeth is one of the most intriguing scenes in the larger story of Jesus' birth. It is so personal, intimate and unlikely. And it also includes some startling claims about what God was about to do through their boys.

These two women suddenly had a special bond. While the angel had directed Mary to Elizabeth, this was Elizabeth's moment of revelation, as the baby "leaped within her" and the Holy Spirit filled her "at the sound of Mary's greeting" (Luke 1:41). Perhaps before anyone else knew of Mary's secret, Elizabeth immediately recognised the momentous event that was beginning within her:

"God has blessed you above all women, and your child is blessed. Why am I so honoured, that the mother of my Lord should visit me? When I heard your greeting, the baby in my womb jumped for joy. You are blessed because you believed that the Lord would do what he said" (Luke 1:42–45).

But this was not the only proclamation of this meeting. Prompted by this extraordinary greeting, Mary did not shy away from the claims Elizabeth had made but broke into a song that for its poetry would readily fit into the book of Psalms and for its intent belongs firmly in the tradition of the Hebrew prophets. She acknowledged the blessings of God and the incredible nature of what was happening to them. And she recognised the goodness and power of God that was working to bring change to the world, announcing a new kingdom of reversal that was about to be realised in their world:

"Oh, how my soul praises the Lord.
How my spirit rejoices in God my Saviour!
For he took notice of his lowly servant girl,
and from now on all generations will call me blessed.
For the Mighty One is holy,
and he has done great things for me.
He shows mercy from generation to generation
to all who fear him.
His mighty arm has done tremendous things!
He has scattered the proud and haughty ones.
He has brought down princes from their thrones
and exalted the humble.
He has filled the hungry with good things
and sent the rich away with empty hands.
He has helped his servant Israel

"He has brought down princes from their thrones and exalted the humble. He has filled the hungry with good things and sent the rich away with empty hands."

and remembered to be merciful.
For he made this promise to our ancestors,
to Abraham and his children forever"
(Luke 1:46–55).

It is a beautiful song of revolution. It is humble and powerful. It is personal and political. It subverts the assumptions and powers of our world. It celebrates God as active, faithful and great. It is the beginning of a holy uprising.

Except that the song seems absurd. These were two peasant women—one old, tired, perennially disappointed, now pregnant and probably feeling the strain in her elderly body; the other an unmarried teenage girl, inexplicably and scandalously pregnant, nervous, perhaps fearful but suddenly bursting with confidence and hope—in a small unnamed village in the hills of Judea. How could they expect their "miracle" boys to begin to undo injustice, to challenge the empires and kings of the day, to change the world and start to set it right? On almost any reading of this story and its anticipated outcomes, it was ridiculous. That both their sons would lose their lives in the process underlines the farce.

Which is why it's also a demonstration of faith and a challenge to our understanding of Jesus.

That Mary's song is recorded, that we know the names of these two women today is remarkable enough. But that this actually was a step towards changing the world has been borne out in history since. Princes have been brought down from their thrones and the humble have indeed been exalted. It is an incomplete project, but this song and this story continue to resonate and bring change in lives and in places of injustice today.

Luke recorded that Mary stayed with Elizabeth for three months (see Luke 1:56) before returning home to face her family and community. In the way the story is told, this suggests that Mary would have left Elizabeth only a short time before her son—who would go on to become the prophet, John the Baptist—was born. Perhaps we see more of their understandings in Zechariah's song after he listened—unable to talk— to some of their many conversations (see Luke 1:67–79). It must have been an important time for both women, as they talked and prayed together, encouraged and helped each other in what they were going through and would confront, and continued to marvel together at the goodness of God and their unlikely roles in His coming kingdom.

When we re-tell the story of the birth of Jesus, we need to remember the perspectives of these two unlikely but "highly favoured" and inspired women. In discovering the newborn King and the kingdom He would establish, we too will learn to sing songs of faithful revolution and holy resistance, which will change us and change the world around us.

12

The Church of the Nativity in Bethlehem is the oldest continuously used church building in the world. It dates from the fourth century, when Roman Emperor Constantine's mother, Helena, visited the Holy Lands to identify locations from the life of Jesus for pilgrimage destinations and church sites. The church is not the shape that we usually associate with a church building; rather it looks like a high pale stone wall that barricades the right-hand-side and end of a wide paved laneway in an L-shape. The point of entry to the church is not obvious, particularly when the area is crowded with pilgrims and tourists, as Manger Square often is.

In Crusader times, the large church door was lowered to reduce the risk of attack, particularly by marauders on horseback. It was later lowered again to its present dimensions. The outlines of the former doorways remain visible in the stonework above. With the top of the doorway only reaching chest height, the church door is currently only able to admit one person at a time. The entrance is known as the "Door of Humility" because everyone entering the church must bow simply to get through the door.

It seems an appropriate way to approach a place of worship or pilgrimage but an even more appropriate way of entering into a place that marks the story of the birth of Jesus.

In re-telling this story, much is often made of the poor conditions into which He was born. Based on the mention of Jesus being "laid . . . in a manger, because there was no lodging available for them" (Luke 2:7), we imagine a stylishly rustic and earthy smelling stable and depict nativity scenes with a farmyard of animals. The more likely setting would have been the lower room of a simple house—a common space sometimes used to shelter animals in the coldest nights of winter, as it does snow occasionally on the Judaean hills—because the main sleeping space in the relative's house was already full of its usual residents and perhaps other visitors. And the manger would most likely have been a large stone feed trough, rather than the neat little wooden box often depicted.

These physical surrounds were given by the angel as a sign to help the shepherds identify the special Baby they were to look for in Bethlehem that night (see Luke 2:12). The place of His birth was in sharp contrast with the nearby Herodium palace from which the king could look out across the hills of Bethlehem. This was an introduction to the kingdom of reversal that Mary had sung about. But the humble circumstances of His birth, the poor working-class family into which He was born, the oppressed and persecuted people that He became part of, while notable, are the lesser humilities of His story.

Far outweighing any of His life circumstances was the reality of His incarnation itself. It is humble for Jesus to have been born poor with all that entails; it is far more humble for God to become human.

In what is believed to have been a hymn of the early church, Paul described this remarkable descent:

> Though he was God,
> he did not think of equality with God
> as something to cling to.
> Instead, he gave up his divine privileges;
> he took the humble position of a slave
> and was born as a human being
> (Philippians 2:6,7).

Paul went on to narrate the subsequent honour paid to Jesus and the universal praise given to Him. This is one of those passages of soaring Christology—the highest praise for who Jesus was and what He did. This was God who risked and sacrificed so much for

"Be humble, thinking of others as better than yourselves. Don't look out only for your own interests, but take an interest in others, too. You must have the same attitude that Christ Jesus had."

humanity and now would be forever worthy of our greatest worship and allegiance.

But we should not miss that Paul's poetic summary of the humility of Jesus was also very practical. He introduced this hymn with these words: "You must have the same attitude that Christ Jesus had" (Philippians 2:5). This is a call to humble lives and humble faith.

But humility is a slippery kind of virtue. Trying to conjure humility within ourselves for its own sake is a frustrating quest. Whenever we notice progress towards humility, we are tempted to be proud of that achievement—and that progress evaporates, possibly even leaving us less humble than where we began. If our focus remains on ourselves, any progress towards humility will be unsustainable. Thus, the need for a "Door of Humility"—something beyond ourselves, perhaps even beyond our culture, that causes us to bow by way of entry.

Humility is not about trying to believe less of ourselves than we know to be true; it is being truthful about what we don't know and who we aren't. Faithful humility comes with looking away from and outside of ourselves—to the story of Jesus and to the stories of others around us. As such, humility is the doorway to faith. And if faith is not humble, it is not faith.

Like the doorway to the Church of the Nativity, the story of the birth of Jesus seems so small—a newborn Child in a distant village so long ago—but it is the humble entrance into a much larger story. We cannot afford to forget that we begin our experience of faith by submitting ourselves to a story, a purpose and a Person that is so much larger than we are. The authentic practice and progress of faith must always bring us back to that small doorway into this larger reality.

In his introduction of the incarnation hymn in Philippians 2, Paul had simple instructions for what living out this story of God-sized humility in our lives would look like: "Don't be selfish; don't try to impress others. Be humble, thinking of others as better than yourselves. Don't look out only for your own interests, but take an interest in others, too. You must have the same attitude that Christ Jesus had" (Philippians 2:3–5).

13

Uncertainty

A few years ago now, I was involved in helping organise a series of annual faith-based creative arts festivals. It was a valuable learning experience and gave me the opportunity to work with a variety of artists and hear some of their thoughts on faithful creativity and creating faithfully. Over the years, I developed quite a reading list around different aspects of these topics.

But, as I talked about and wrestled with our call to faithfully seek out and create beauty and goodness in our world, one of the frustrations that grew in me was the seeming disparity between the imagery and language of the two dominant aesthetic realities in our world. Too often, we witness violence, tragedy, hunger and horror, then try to respond by talking about flowers and sunsets, butterflies and rainbows. Even when we talk about love—"the greatest of these" (1 Corinthians 13:13)—it can feel so easily overwhelmed by its opposites: fear, hate and death.

Why do goodness and beauty, hope and love seem so flimsy, ephemeral and uncertain? When trying to argue that these are more important, powerful and sustainable realities, our language seems to let us down. In short, good so often seems weaker than evil.

Until we remember that such weakness is the way of God.

As we have seen, the dramatic imagery of Revelation 12 pictures a confrontation between a newborn baby and a great destructive dragon (see verses 1–5). It is not a comforting image, particularly as we are drawn into the story and recognise God's way of engaging in this conflict. It appears doomed to fail.

In the story of the birth of Jesus, God's great act of intervention in the history and trajectory of our world played out in the uncertainty, messiness and humanity of pregnancy and childbirth. Then God's plan was still at risk, threatened by the fragility of infancy, the hardships of poverty and the brute force of subjugation by Herod's murderous soldiers (see Matthew 2:13–18). Like much of human history, the times in which Jesus lived were dangerous and difficult: "Life was slow, hard and short."[1] Theologians debate the degree of risk that God undertook, whether the plan could have gone wrong, whether Jesus could have failed. While many of the details and hypotheticals remain mysteries, it seems there was real peril for God Himself in this project of incarnation and intervention.

And from most perspectives, it was not a glorious triumph. Jesus would arouse opposition and division. His life would be short and end brutally, and it would bring pain to those who were closest to Him. As Simeon warned Mary when she and Joseph presented the eight-day-old Jesus at the temple:

"This child is destined to cause many in Israel to fall, and many others to rise. He has been sent as a sign from God, but many will oppose him. As a result, the deepest thoughts of many hearts will be revealed. And a sword will pierce your very soul" (Luke 2:34, 35).

As such, becoming a baby seems an unlikely and risky way for God to intervene in our world. But if uncertain hope was good enough for God, it should be enough for us. Further, our understanding of faith maintains that this humble and gentle posture is most God-like, the most true, the most poetic and the most powerful.

But there are other elements of the story that underline this counter-intuitive aesthetic of God and His ways. For example, theologian Walter Brueggemann contrasts the Roman emperor's census decree with the angels' announcement of the birth of Jesus:

The rulers had decreed a census and all the managing ways that went with it, but a census never led to energy or newness. This new one from God could not and

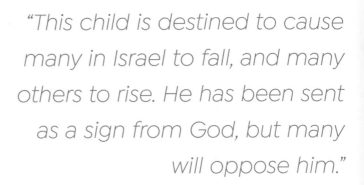

"This child is destined to cause many in Israel to fall, and many others to rise. He has been sent as a sign from God, but many will oppose him."

would not be counted. The grim holding action of census was penetrated by the unscheduled and unextrapolated song of angels who sing a new song for a new king. There is no way to begin this new narrative except by a new song in the mouth of angels, authorised from the throne of God. . . . The beginning is with a *song* that stands in conflict with the *decree*. All the old history is by decree, but the new history begins another way.[2]

In Luke's telling of the story, both the decree and the song claimed the attention of "all people" (compare Luke 2:1, 3 and 2:10, 14), but one was an action of bureaucratic oppression and economic exploitation, the other a celebration of joy, glory and peace.

In the history of our world, songs are usually less powerful than decrees. But in the way of God, a song can overwhelm a decree, a baby can confront an empire, an infant can overcome a dragon, love can conquer fear, hate and death, and somehow a flimsy beauty is more enduring than a horrific headline.

In the vocabulary and practice of faith, an uncertain hope is always more important than a hopeless certainty. But this challenges our human instinct towards certainty, even though many of our certainties tend to be bleak. We are uncomfortable when we are uncertain, so we are often tempted to accept bland certainty, rather than embracing the risks and possibilities of imagination, creativity and hope. It is true that there are things we can know, realities we can be certain of, but the things that matter most cannot be forced or decreed. Uncertainty is an element in many of the things that make us most human—and what made God most human in the story of the birth of Jesus.

We still need new language and better imagination to talk about and create beauty and justice and goodness in our world. But we can begin by reclaiming the language that we have—and the stories and the songs that God has used to speak and act in the past history of our world. And this new history began with the birth of Jesus.

1. I borrowed this summary from my friend Kayle de Waal, *Hearing the Way*, Signs Publishing, 2019, page 22.

2. Walter Brueggemann, *The Prophetic Imagination* (Second Edition), Fortress Press, 2001, pages 102–3.

14

Wonder

High in the central space of the Church of the Holy Sepulchre in the Old City of Jerusalem, each of the four pillars that support one of the church's grey domes is illustrated with paintings of one of the writers of the New Testament's four gospels: Matthew, Mark, Luke and John. As the writer who gives us the most details of the story of the birth of Jesus, this traditional representation of Luke is intriguing. He is pictured sitting on a terrace; his book is laid aside and he holds a paintbrush in his hand as he seems to be putting the finishing touches on a portrait of Mary and a young Jesus.

Despite no evidence in the Bible itself for Luke being an artist, this possibility catches my imagination. Imagine if there were original paintings of Jesus, His disciples and other characters in the story. And imagine if "The Gospel According to Luke" was originally an illustrated biography. Like so many traditions, this idea grew out of proportion and, at the height of medieval Christianity, churches across the Christian world claimed hundreds of paintings credited to "St Luke".

It is interesting to re-read Luke's gospel story with an eye for his descriptions of scenes, people and stories. Of the gospel writers, Luke dedicated the most space not only to telling the story of the birth of Jesus but also to setting the scene for it. His lengthy first chapter introduces us to a number of different people who each add to our anticipation of something about to happen. Luke took the time to build a context of people and relationships, hopes and fears.

Luke's story of the birth of Jesus and the surrounding events was coloured particularly with the emotions of the surprised participants. As previously noted, one of their first and most obvious emotional responses was fear. This seems appropriate when we have angels appearing with talk of unexplainable pregnancies and a coming king. Such announcements were religiously, politically and socially dangerous. They were also puzzling and eminently unlikely. Mary's second response to the angel was described like this: "Confused and disturbed, Mary tried to think what the angel could mean" (Luke 1:29).

But as the story progressed, these responses and emotions began to change. Not all the questions that Mary, Joseph, Zechariah and Elizabeth and the other participants who became part of the story asked or might have asked were resolved. The uncertainty remained. But there was a change of feeling. Where fear was a first reaction, the realisation grew that something good was happening among them. And fear increasingly became wonder—perhaps a holy fear, with the two not so far apart as emotions but diverging greatly in trajectory and consequence.

The perpetual disappointment of the barren Elizabeth turned to joy in her own motherhood and the recognition of Mary's child, and Zechariah overcame the silence that resulted from his stubbornness to affirm the angel's name for his unexpected son and celebrate with family. It was something that could not be contained in their home: "Awe fell upon the whole neighbourhood, and the news of what had happened spread throughout the Judean hills. Everyone who heard about it reflected on these events and asked, 'What will this child turn out to be?'" (Luke 1:65, 66).

In a similar transformation, the fear of the shepherds outside Bethlehem compelled them to go to see with their own eyes what the angel had told them about. What they discovered was not something they could keep to themselves: "After seeing him, the shepherds told everyone what had happened and what the angel had said to them about this child. All who heard the shepherds' story were astonished, but Mary kept all these things in her heart and thought about them

"Awe fell upon the whole neighbourhood. . . . Everyone who heard about it reflected on these events and asked, 'What will this child turn out to be?'"

often" (Luke 2:17–19). Progressing from fear to wonder, not only did these rough working men become the first human proclaimers of the newborn King, they added to Mary's sense of wonder and her increasing understanding of this thing that she was so privileged to be part of.

Mary would have another such experience when she and Joseph made the customary sacrifices for the birth of a child when Jesus was eight days old. Due to the census decree, Mary and Joseph were not far from the temple in Jerusalem and it was there they went to offer the sacrifices. Although the trip is much more complicated today with security walls between Israeli and Palestinian territories, Bethlehem is only 8 kilometres (5 miles) from Jerusalem, meaning this was probably only a day trip for the new parents.

In the temple, Mary and Joseph met the enthusiastic proclamations and praise of Simeon and Anna, two elderly individuals who somehow recognised Jesus as the One they had been waiting for their whole lives. They had a sense of wonder that was contagious, stoking wonder in Mary and Joseph themselves: "Jesus' parents were amazed at what was being said about him" (Luke 2:33).

Many mothers keep some kind of scrapbook of the milestones and achievements of their children, but in recording the story of Jesus' birth, Luke paused for a moment to reflect with Mary about the wondrous things she had experienced: "And his mother stored all these things in her heart" (Luke 2:51).

Such depictions remind us of the human experience of those who were most closely connected with the birth of Jesus. Their fear gave way to wonder. It seemed dangerous, but they came to recognise that what was happening was good. And they also recognised that while it was their profound personal experience, it also mattered somehow to the whole world.

Perhaps this was part of the insight that Luke the (possible) painter brought to his storytelling: "To see things is to enhance your sense of wonder both for the singular pattern of your own experience, and for the meta-patterns that shape all experience."[1] Perhaps we too can experience wonder in this story—for ourselves and for our world and its people throughout history. So let's treat them like Mary did, keeping these stories in our hearts and thinking about them often.

1. David Bayles and Ted Orland, *Art & Fear: Observations on the Perils (and Rewards) of Artmaking*, The Image Continuum, 1993, page 101.

15

Generosity

Among the many traditions that have grown up around our contemporary celebration of the Christmas season, gift-giving has come to dominate. Unfortunately, this is not always for the best reasons. For many sectors of the shopping industry, the end-of-year holiday season has come to represent more than a third of annual sales, so there are strong economic interests and large advertising budgets encouraging people to spend "money they can't afford on presents you neither need nor want"—as Frederick Buechner put it.[1]

Many of us feel the pressure to give gifts and the stress of trying to think of gifts that will be appreciated by family, friends and others we might feel obligated to give to. And then there is the financial strain that is common at this time of year and in its aftermath.

On the other hand, we have also felt the gratification when we have been able to give a gift to someone we care about that is something they need or want or that expresses our appreciation for them and their contribution to our lives. And these gifts do not need to be the most expensive or even creative; at their best, they are a way of saying thank you and showing that we care.

When we get this attitude right, we can recognise the truth in a statement that Paul quoted from Jesus—which, intriguingly, is not included in any of the four gospels—"It is more blessed to give than to receive" (Acts 20:35). Of course, this principle is not primarily about Christmas, but it is relevant to Christmas because it is a time of year when we tend to be more focused on giving.

And, unlike many of the traditions around Christmas, the practice of giving has some presence in the story of the birth of Jesus, albeit with further layers of tradition grown around it. The magi—or wise men—"from eastern lands" (Matthew 2:1) arrived in Jerusalem sometime after the birth of Jesus, seeking the newborn king of the Jews. Directed to Bethlehem, "they entered the house and saw the child with his mother, Mary, and they bowed down and worshipped him. Then they opened their treasure chests and gave him gifts of gold, frankincense, and myrrh" (Matthew 2:11).

Their three gifts have led to the assumption of three wise men and their story has been imagined, embellished and explained in countless ways. While the expensive and exotic gifts seem out of character with much of the rest of the story and its characters, and although "no broad historical precedent exists for this link"[2] and Christmas gift-giving is probably only a more recent tradition, the magi's example links gift-giving with the story of the birth of Jesus.

However, even when considered in their best light, the gifts of the magi pale in comparison with the ultimate gift in the story of the birth of Jesus: "For this is how God loved the world: He *gave* his one and only Son" (John 3:16).

The various writers of the New Testament would struggle to express and explain the magnitude of God's "inexpressible" or "unspeakable" gift: "Thank God for this gift too wonderful for words!" (2 Corinthians 9:15). They often used the word *grace* to describe God's generosity—giving to humanity much more than we deserve. And they urged that the generosity of God they had experienced and come to understand in Jesus was the basis for relying on His overwhelming goodness and provision in all aspects of our lives: "Since he did not spare even his own Son but gave him up for us all, won't he also give us everything else?" (Romans 8:32).

This was also the basis for a generous attitude and way of living in our world. The Gift Himself—Jesus—would teach His disciples that they were to "give as freely as you have received!" (Matthew 10:8). But this command includes a significant precursor to genuine generosity: we must first be willing to receive.

"Thank God for this gift too wonderful for words!"

Giving does not always come from the purest of motives. It can be a response of guilt for the excesses and shortcomings of our lives. There are those who are willing to exploit such unease in coaxing us to give, even with good intentions. One of the clichés of the Christmas season is that it is "the time for giving." Another is that because many of us have so much we should take the opportunity to give to those who have less than us. There is truth in such statements, but they are often not the best motivation for giving.

Such an attitude can also reduce giving to an act of power. We give because we can or because we wish to think of ourselves—or be seen by others—as generous. In short, even our best acts can so easily become more about us than any would-be beneficiaries.

This is why we need to learn how to receive. When stripped of Christmas' contrived good will, the story of the birth of Jesus is primarily about receiving the gift of Jesus. While we know so little about the motivations and experiences of the magi, it is possible that if they merely delivered their gifts and returned "to their own country by another route" (Matthew 2:12), they could have missed the point of their quest. When we learn how to receive with the humility that comes from truly recognising our need of grace, our other attitudes, actions and motivations begin to change.

So as we re-tell the story of the birth of Jesus, we ought to spend time thinking about receiving this Gift and what this means for our lives. As much as possible, shift the focus from the giving and the getting. Instead practise the art of receiving; practise humility, gratitude and grace. Allow the Gift of God, His generosity and His promises to change the world in us and around us. Yes, giving is good, but it is also "blessed to receive"—and receiving is the foundation for the best kinds of giving.

1. See Chapter 6.

2. Paul Ringel, "Why Children Get Gifts on Christmas: A History," *The Atlantic*, December 25, 2015, <www.theatlantic.com/business/arhive/2015/12/why-people-give-christmas-gifts/421908/>.

16

Peace

One of the most common sentiments in the cards and carols of the Christmas season is peace. It is biblical—based in the stories around Jesus' birth—but might also seem one of the most wishful and sometimes ironic.

Peace was a key theme in the celebratory song of the angels who announced Jesus' birth to the shepherds outside Bethlehem. You'll often see their song on Christmas cards in the older English text on which many Christmas traditions are based:

> Glory to God in the highest,
> and on earth peace,
> good will toward men
> (Luke 2:14, KJV).

But given the political and social context in which He was born, the tumult and division that seemed part of His life and that of so many of His followers after His death, the litany of wars that have been attributed to religion in the 2000 years since, and the reputation of Israel and the wider Middle East for violence and conflict even today, the promise of peace can seem like misplaced sentimentality or even a tragic lie. If the birth of Jesus was to bring a new age of peace, it has seemed a failure for much of our subsequent history.

Yet this was not merely an over-exuberance on the part of the angels—and this was not a new theme in the story. In celebrating the unlikely birth of his new son, Zechariah the priest concluded his song of praise with the expectation that something even larger was about to happen, something that would lead to greater peace: "Because of God's tender mercy, the morning light from heaven is about to break upon us, to give light to those who sit in darkness and in the shadow of death, and to guide us to the path of peace" (Luke 1:78, 79).

But neither was this an original sentiment. Zechariah was drawing on the old and holy writings of his own tradition. In what has become one of the best known prophecies of the birth of Jesus from the Hebrew scriptures and another one of those Christmas card verses, the prophet Isaiah wrote:

> For unto us a child is born, unto us a son is given:
> and the government shall be upon his shoulder:
> and his name shall be called Wonderful,
> Counsellor, The mighty God,
> The everlasting Father, The Prince of Peace
> (Isaiah 9:6, KJV).

These are bold claims about a newborn baby, but as we have already considered, these claims are at the heart of the Bible's story about Jesus and who He was—before, at and after His birth. Yet "Prince of Peace" is a new title and one that does not fit so well with much of our understanding of history.

Helpfully, Isaiah went further to develop this theme: "His government and its peace will never end. He will rule with fairness and justice from the throne of his ancestor David for all eternity. The passionate commitment of the Lord of Heaven's Armies will make this happen!" (Isaiah 9:7). This verse highlights aspects of this promised peace that are important, if we are not to dismiss it either as merely a noble seasonal sentiment or failed wishful thinking.

True peace is not merely the absence of conflict. Those seeking superficial peace may be content to put an end to obvious fighting or unrest. And for those in war zones, situations of abuse or inter-

"Because of God's tender mercy, the morning light from heaven is about to break upon us, to give light to those who sit in darkness and in the shadow of death, and to guide us to the path of peace."

personal tension, an end to the overt violence and hostilities is a good thing in itself. The guns falling silent must be an important and necessary first step. But a much deeper peace comes with justice and reconciliation, healing and restoration.

In some of the best moments of human history, the story and teachings of Jesus have been among the catalysts for this deeper kind of peace. People of faith and people of good will have worked for the fairness and justice that characterise the rule of this Child. Peace has been made in some corners of our world and its history by the influence of the Prince of Peace.

However, this is so obviously and tragically an incomplete project: "The world-transforming peace that the angel declared to the shepherds is only found in bits and fragments now. Its eternal fulfilment is to be found only in the future of God."[1] The promise of the angels and of Isaiah and Zechariah before them is also yet to be realised.

This is the far larger promise of peace found in the story of the birth of Jesus. It offers and invites reconciliation for the broken relationships between all people and between humanity and God: "For Christ himself has brought peace to us" (Ephesians 2:14). This is not the one-dimensional "silent night" of snowy Christmas cards and carols, on which the whole world supposedly paused in wonder to greet the newborn Baby, but the proclamation that something wholly different had come into the world and a new human reality had begun:

> Here is the forward thrust of Advent . . . the heralding announcement of the arriving God. The note that is struck is sounded from the future. We are not looking backward sentimentally to a baby; we are looking forward to the only One in whom the promise of peace will someday be fulfilled.[2]

In His life and teaching, Jesus sometimes did not sound like a preacher of peace. He was blunt about the trouble, the polarisation and the persecution that would be experienced by those who would follow Him. His execution and that of almost every one of His disciples over the following decades bitterly demonstrated His point. But He also taught peace, in response to those enemies, as an attitude of a faithful heart and mind, and as a tangible expectation for our world and its future. "I have told you all this so that you may have peace in me," Jesus told His followers. "Here on earth you will have many trials and sorrows. But take heart, because I have overcome the world" (John 16:33).

It is not that those Christmas cards and carols are wrong. It is perhaps that they—and we—don't take this promise of peace seriously enough. The birth of the Prince of Peace offers a deeper, more transformative and more forever kind of peace than we often allow ourselves to imagine or to work towards in the world today.

1. Fleming Rutledge, *Advent: The Once & Future Coming of Jesus*, Eerdmans Publishing Co, 2018, page 339.

2. ibid, page 342.

17

Love

If we have tendency to over-sentimentalise the idea of peace in the Christmas season, we have a tendency to over-sentimentalise love almost all the time and just about everywhere. In so much of popular culture, love is a dominant theme. Although largely undefined, it is generally understood as some kind of warm feeling towards someone or something. Perhaps part of the challenge is that we tend to overuse a single English word to cover so many different affections, likes, desires, attachments and commitments.

This limitation of our language becomes a challenge when we start trying to talk about the love of God or even that "God is love" (1 John 4:8). While a statement such as this seems so definitive, understood as coming from one of Jesus' closest followers, it can leave us with so many more questions about what that actually means. The language lets us down.

But there is another way of talking about love, offering a more external understanding, expression and even measure of what it means. Talking in this way urges that, while emotions and feelings are part of its motivation, love is more about transformative action that makes tangible differences for the recipient or object of that love. And when love is expressed towards our neighbours and other people in our communities, nations and world, it makes a difference. As justice activist and Black American leader Cornel West has often been quoted as saying, "Justice is what love looks like in public."

So when we ask questions about what God's love looks like for us and our world, we should look for how God has acted towards us.

And the Bible consistently points to a central action that encapsulates God's active and transformative love: "For this is how God *loved* the world: He gave his one and only Son" (John 3:16). Reflecting on this pre-eminent expression of God's love, while not diminishing the truth of West's original statement, we might adapt his formulation: "Jesus is what God's love looks like in public," or zooming out a little further, "Jesus is what God's love looks like in the history of our world."

Rather than a broad and vague feeling of affection or good will, God's expression of love is so specific that if we wish to understand His love we begin with the story of the birth of Jesus. So are you looking for the love of God in the world around us? If so, "You will find a baby wrapped snugly in strips of cloth, lying in a manger" (Luke 2:12)—as the angels directed the shepherds outside Bethlehem. This is the simplicity and the counter-intuitive complexity of what the love of God looks like for us.

Those New Testament writers who took up the task of reflecting on and explaining what happened in the story of Jesus repeatedly emphasised that what they had seen, experienced and reported to their readers was a revelation of God—what He is like and how He regards us and our world. For example, Paul would urge that the event of Jesus' birth demonstrated something that is so much more powerful than the worst circumstances and challenges of our lives. This was urgent and important for many of the people he was writing to, who were facing persecution and the threat of death because of their identification with Him:

> Can anything ever separate us from Christ's love? Does it mean he no longer loves us if we have trouble or calamity, or are persecuted, or hungry, or destitute, or in danger, or threatened with death? . . . I am convinced that nothing can ever separate us from God's love. Neither death nor life, neither angels nor demons, neither our fears for today nor our worries about tomorrow—not even the powers of hell can separate us

"For this is how God loved the world: He gave his one and only Son."

from God's love. No power in the sky above or in the earth below—indeed, nothing in all creation will ever be able to separate us from the love of God that is revealed in Christ Jesus our Lord (Romans 8:35–39).

Somehow all our questions about God—to the extent that they can be revealed to human minds and probably not always as directly as we might like—find their answer in Jesus. So if the essential nature of God is love, then Jesus is the light that shines that love into the otherwise darkness of our lives and our world (see John 1:5).

Of course, such an expression of love does not happen by accident. Love requires intentionality. Love requires perseverance and endurance.[1] Not only was this action something hoped for and anticipated in our world, the Bible describes God as One whose love for humanity was so important that He developed a plan for restoring our relationships, even before they were broken, even before we were born, even before our world began. Paul explained it like this: "I was chosen to explain to everyone this mysterious plan that God, the Creator of all things, had kept secret from the beginning. . . . This was his eternal plan, which he carried out through Christ Jesus our Lord" (Ephesians 3:9–11).

As we have noted previously, in Paul's sometimes convoluted

explanations of this great plan of God's love, he would drop his scholarly prose from time to time, in favour of more poetic praise or pastoral prayer. The second half of this third chapter of his letter to the church in Ephesus was one of those outbursts:

> May you have the power to understand, as all God's people should, how wide, how long, how high, and how deep his love is. May you experience the love of Christ, though it is too great to understand fully. Then you will be made complete with all the fullness of life and power that comes from God (Ephesians 3:18, 19).

It keeps coming back to Jesus. Jesus is what God's love looks like in our world. In a real sense, His birth was the arrival of God's love in a new way. The story of His birth was the beginning of the plan on the ground, in flesh and blood, in a specific time and place, in history and community, in all its complexity and simplicity—in love.

1. See 1 Corinthians 13 for a fuller expression of love at its best.

18

Lowly

As a writer, there are certain words that catch my attention—and I have favourites. It might be how the letters fit together, how the word sounds when spoken or perhaps simply the meaning that can be conveyed with one good, well-placed word. *Lowly* is one of those words—and one that seems to be heard only occasionally—perhaps most often in Christmas stories and carols.

Conspicuously, this description appears in Mary's song of praise when visiting Elizabeth: "Oh, how my soul praises the Lord. How my spirit rejoices in God my Saviour! For he took notice of his *lowly* servant girl, and from now on all generations will call me blessed" (Luke 1:46–48). In her song, Mary pointed out a refrain in God's interactions with our world and its people, contrasting His concern for the lowly with His judgment of the proud, the rich and the powerful.

It is a theme that continues through the story of the birth of Jesus. Not only are we directed to focus our attention on a peasant girl and an ageing, barren woman in the hills of Judea, the story contrasts the power and decrees of Roman rulers and the concerns of the political and religious leaders in Jerusalem with what God was doing and about to do away from the headlines of the day—almost off-screen, except for Luke's narration.

The angels did not announce Jesus' birth to the religious scholars in the temple but to a few ordinary shepherds out in a field. And it would have been a jolt even to their expectations and sensibilities when the angel directed them to look for "the Saviour . . . the

Messiah, the Lord" (Luke 2:11) in a manger—a feeding trough for domestic animals. The magi were surprised not to find the newborn King in a palace in the city. Jesus' parents were shown to be poor by the offerings they brought to the temple, with pigeons an alternative sacrifice for a new mother who "cannot afford to bring a lamb" (Leviticus 12:8). And it was not the officious priest on duty in the temple who recognised who Jesus was, instead it was left to old Simeon and the widowed Anna to prophesy over and praise the Baby.

The story of the birth of Jesus is a narrative of the unlikely. It seems that the poor, the humble and the marginalised were preferred at every turn in this story:

> Only the humble believe Him and rejoice that God is so free and so marvellous that He does wonders where people despair, that He takes what is little and lowly and makes it marvellous. And that is the wonder of all wonders, that God loves the lowly. . . . God is not ashamed of the lowliness of human beings. God marches right in. He chooses people as His instruments and performs His wonders where one would least expect them. God is near to lowliness; He loves the lost, the neglected, the unseemly, the excluded, the weak and broken.[1]

We are assured that God loves all people, even the whole world. But without diminishing His love for others, He has a particular preference, concern and love for the lowly. This focus would persist throughout Luke's telling of the story of Jesus, in which he builds from these humble beginnings to describe a humble teacher who would come to be recognised as a humble Messiah and, in His death and resurrection, a humble Saviour. In all of this, His preference and place were among the lowly, poor and excluded.

In Luke's record of Jesus' visit to the synagogue in His hometown of Nazareth, Jesus read from the prophecies of Isaiah to announce the focus of His ministry and work:

"This foolish plan of God is wiser than the wisest of human plans, and God's weakness is stronger than the greatest of human strength."

> The Spirit of the Lord is upon me, for he has anointed me to bring Good News to the poor. He has sent me to proclaim that captives will be released, that the blind will see, that the oppressed will be set free, and that the time of the Lord's favour has come (Luke 4:18, 19).

And He fulfilled Isaiah's description in His practical ministry of proximity, healing and preaching among the poor and the outcasts, and offered this as evidence of who He was (see Luke 7:18–23).

Whereas Matthew's version of the Beatitudes—the counter-intuitive constitution of the alternative kingdom Jesus was announcing—has allowed many earnest preachers to spiritualise their focus and impacts, Luke was concerned to not allow us to so readily sidestep their tangible preference for the lowly:

> God blesses you who are poor,
>> for the Kingdom of God is yours.
>
> God blesses you who are hungry now,
>> for you will be satisfied.
>
> God blesses you who weep now,
>> for in due time you will laugh (Luke 6:20, 21).

In Jesus—in the story and circumstances of His birth, as well as in His ministry, life and death—God "descended to our lowly world" (Ephesians 4:9) and repeatedly demonstrated that He is especially near to the humble within our world. This is good news when we experience times in our lives when we are or feel beaten down, but it must also challenge our understanding and practice of who and what are valuable in the world around us. Insisting that specific needs and lives matter is consistent with God's preference for the lowly. Those who suffer most from poverty, injustice and oppression receive God's particular concern—and so they demand ours.

The story of the birth of Jesus is a template for living in our world differently. People, power and position matter differently in the light that shone around the shepherds outside the village of Bethlehem that night:

> This foolish plan of God is wiser than the wisest of human plans, and God's weakness is stronger than the greatest of human strength. . . . God chose things the world considers foolish in order to shame those who think they are wise. And he chose things that are powerless to shame those who are powerful. God chose things despised by the world, things counted as nothing at all, and used them to bring to nothing what the world considers important (1 Corinthians 1:25–28).

In reflecting on the story of Jesus' birth, *lowly* is a word worth keeping in mind.

1. Dietrich Bonhoeffer, *God is in the Manger: Reflections on Advent and Christmas,* Westminster John Knox Press, 2010, page 22.

19

Outsiders

For their prominence in many re-tellings of the Christmas stories, the magi have only a relatively brief cameo in Matthew's narration of the story. And, while so many nativity scenes like to include them for additional visual interest, it seems highly unlikely they arrived in Bethlehem on the night Jesus was born. More commonly referred to as wise men—and, of course, tradition has dictated that there were three of them—these mysterious visitors were also described as "royal astrologers."[1] They were mysterious and exotic and seemed to catch the attention of the inhabitants and leaders in Jerusalem by their arrival and the awkward questions they asked (see Matthew 2:3).

There has been much conjecture and imagination about where the magi came from and what motivated their search for the newborn king. Some have suggested that they might have been students of the writings of the Babylon-based Hebrew scholar, politician and prophet Daniel of some 500 years earlier. Other have theorised that they were ancient astronomers who assumed that a new and unexpected star would herald a new power and were curious to find out what this might mean.

And then there was the star itself, which they reported had led them to Jerusalem. After their inquiries with the political and religious leaders of the nation, "the star they had seen in the east guided them to Bethlehem. It went ahead of them and stopped over the place where the child was. When they saw the star, they were filled with joy!" (Matthew 2:9, 10). The story described how these strange visitors gave their gifts and worshipped the Child—but the Bible story does not give more details or explain further.

Among the various characters in the story of the birth of Jesus, I have a soft spot for the magi. For more than 25 years, a number of churches in Melbourne have worked together to produce an interactive, entertaining and thoughtful re-telling of the story of Jesus' birth. Called Road to Bethlehem, it has grown to regularly attract more than 15,000 guests over four nights each year. It has also been adapted and performed in other locations around Australia and New Zealand. As one of more than 300 volunteer cast, crew and team members, I have played each one of the three different "wise man" roles over a number of years, acting in the same two scenes as many as 15 times each night as different groups move through the story.

In these roles, I have had many opportunities to reflect on these strange characters, the nature of their quest and the role they played in Jesus' story. In this re-telling of the story, as the wise men exit their first scene, they are led to the palace by the local Roman centurion, while the dramatic action continues in the Jerusalem marketplace. Many times I have heard the dialogue continue as we walk away, commenting on our dangerous questions about a newborn king and our impending audience with Herod: "I wouldn't want to be in their sandals . . ."

But the wise men offer an important perspective on the story. I have imagined them as learned men who don't fit with the more provincial characters in Jerusalem, but who are puzzled and disappointed by the unwitting ignorance and self-interested plotting they encounter.

There is a recurring motif in the stories of the Bible of outsiders who contribute significantly to the progress of God's interactions with those who assume they are His people. It is too easy for those who seem chosen by God to imagine that the story is solely about them. But, every so often, unexpected outsiders appear to somehow bless or assist the people and to alert or even warn of what God was doing among them.

"It went ahead of them and stopped over the place where the child was. When they saw the star, they were filled with joy!"

In this case, the magi were the first proclaimers of the good news of the birth of Jesus—the new king of the Jews—to the political and religious leaders and all the people of Jerusalem (see Matthew 2:3, 4). We can only imagine how the story of Jesus might have been different if the magi's questions had been taken more seriously by the Jewish religious leaders and people of Jerusalem. We can also wonder if there might have been some who did hear the questions, made their own inquiries and, as a result, might have become followers of Jesus when He began His public ministry some 30 years later.

The other important role that characters such as the magi play in the stories of the Bible is to remind the people—and the readers—that God's story and action in the world are bigger than had been anticipated. Because they seem to appear from nowhere, we can forget that there is a whole other story that has led them to that point. Of course, there were likely months of travel to arrive in Jerusalem, but there was also the study and reflection that led them to look and ultimately prompted their journey and their worship (see Matthew 2:11). The story also makes clear that they were open to the leading of God—"When it was time to leave, they returned to their own country by another route, for God had warned them in a dream not to return to Herod" (Matthew 2:12)—so we can surmise that He had led and guided them to that point.

The story of the magi demonstrates that there is a place for outsiders in the story of God, and sometimes this is more faithfully filled than by some assumed insiders. Not only are outsiders invited and welcomed, they are necessary for some elements of the story. While it seems that their quest triggered the murderous rage of King Herod (see Matthew 2:16), we should not hold them responsible for the way in which he responded to their inquiries. He might have chosen to genuinely join them in their desire to worship the Child (see Matthew 2:8). Instead, some traditions suggest that their expensive and exotic gifts might have provided the financial means for Joseph, Mary and Jesus during their time living as refugees in Egypt.

Offering so much more than a touch of the exotic in a nativity scene or Christmas pageant, the magi remind us that in the story of God we are all outsiders, in a sense. But His is an open story. Whoever we might be and wherever we are from, our story can become part of His story—if we choose.

1. See Matthew 2:1, footnote.

20

Christmas

Writing to a friend in late 1958, Oxford scholar and Christian author C S Lewis commented on the all-too-common ignorance regarding the true story behind Christmas with "a story which puts the contrast between our feast of the Nativity and all this ghastly 'Xmas' racket at its lowest. My brother heard a woman on a bus say, as the bus passed a church with a Crib outside it, 'Oh Lor'! They bring religion into everything. Look—they're dragging it even into Christmas now!'"[1]

As the busyness, frenzy and pressure builds towards the Christmas holiday, this can feel like the reality of Christmas today. Even for those of us with the best of intentions, Jesus can come to feel like one more thing to think about and feel guilty about not doing as well as we feel we should. And, of course, Christmas in many parts of the world today has little to do with the story of Jesus—to such a degree that it might feel like the story is being dragged into or added onto the traditions of the secular season of shopping and celebration. But, like many of our modern traditions, they really aren't as old as we assume.

Christmas as we know it today in western countries and in places where Christmas has been adopted by their influence is largely a creation of the American advertising industry in the 19th and 20th centuries. This influence in popular western culture has been aided by *A Christmas Carol* by Charles Dickens, which has been perennially popular and never out of print since it was first published in 1843. These voices offered a secular season of good will and giving, characterised by seasonal food, gifts, decorations and lights, and secular Christmas songs as much as sacred Christmas carols.

Similarly, much of the religious celebration of Christmas is recorded in the development of these Christmas carols, as hymns and songs that reflect on the story of the birth of Jesus. Yet most of the popular carols can be dated only to the Protestant Reformation of the 16th century and many of them were written in step with the development of the modern Christmas in the 19th century. Even Handel's *Messiah*, often performed as part of the Christmas season, was written in the 18th century, relatively recent in the context of 2000 years of Christian history.

The traditional Christmas season of Advent and "feast of the Nativity"—as Lewis defended it—is much older but also has limited connection to the story of Jesus' birth. There is no directive in the Bible itself that mandates or even encourages the celebration of a festival to mark Jesus' birth date. And, despite how the carols would portray the event, it seems unlikely that the census would have been decreed or that shepherds would have been out in their fields at night in the depth of winter in late December. There are some who have urged that the date was linked to the pagan festival of the Winter Solstice in the Roman world, but this is now rejected by historians who offer other explanations of how ancient Christians might have settled on December 25.[2]

Putting all of this together, the Christmas that is celebrated in all its different aspects and forms in the world today has little to do with the story of the birth of Jesus. It is a conglomeration of many historical influences, cultural traditions, religious customs, secular folklore, commercial advertising and other vested economic interests.

For someone wanting to re-tell the story of Jesus' birth, it can sometimes feel like the noise of Christmas so readily drowns out the story of Jesus. But somehow it seems appropriate that Jesus feels almost like an outsider in His own story: "He came into the very world he created, but the world didn't recognise him. He came to his own people, and even they rejected him" (John 1:10, 11).

"He came into the very world he created, but the world didn't recognise him. He came to his own people, and even they rejected him."

Perhaps, consistent with the realities and impact of the story of the birth of Jesus, the confused and assorted origins of Christmas might be kind of the point. That, because of the incarnation of Jesus, everything can be redeemed. That we can begin practising today the promise of Revelation that "the world has now become the Kingdom of our Lord and of his Christ, and he will reign forever and ever" (Revelation 11:15). And that this was enacted not in the hermetically sealed purity of a distant heaven but amid the mess and the ugliness, the dirt and blood, the profanity and the obliviousness of our world.

That's what incarnation is.

It is not like we need to protect the purity of God. While the angels sang "Glory in the highest" (see Luke 2:14), the embodied truth of the story of Jesus' birth was that Glory was now found among the lowest. The risk is that we keep this story too clean. The truth of Christmas is a jarring revolution in our understanding of the nature and reputation of God. It is far more disturbing for God to become human than a confused and over-commercialised celebration to become a time to remember and celebrate this remarkable story of God and His love.

Because of the ambiguities and some of the darker assumptions about the origins and motivations of Christmas, some people think they need to reject Christmas and resist any and all of the trappings and traditions of the season. But what makes us different—in the most worthwhile sense—at this time of year is not that we don't celebrate Christmas but that we celebrate Jesus and all that He means to us. In Jesus, God was found in the back blocks of humanity, and the story of Jesus offers redemption, transformation and hope to all people, to all cultures, to all history.

Amid the echoes of ancient religious festivals, the syrup of Christmas carolling and the din of a hyper-commercialised secular holiday, we discover, re-tell and celebrate the story of the birth of Jesus. This is incarnation. This is redemption. This is how God works.

1. C S Lewis, *Letters to an American Lady,* William B Eerdmans Publishing Co, 1971, page 80.

2. For example, see Andrew McGowan, "How December 25 Became Christmas," *Bible History Daily*, December 10, 2019, <www.biblicalarchaeology.org/daily/biblical-topics/new-testament/how-december-25-became-christmas/>.

21

Some years ago, my wife and I were invited to join a tour group that a friend was leading to Israel and the Palestinian Territories, focused on visiting key places in the Bible's stories. I was hesitant at first, but my wife's interest and the enthusiasm of other friends who had visited these places—or wanted to visit—coaxed me towards saying yes.

A few months later, our first stop was four days in and around the walled Old City in Jerusalem, where my uncertainty and questions returned immediately. Amid the historical and holy places, the competing church bells and calls to prayers, the seemingly endless markets, the crowds of tourists, pilgrims and worshippers, I was still wrestling with why I was there and what I hoped to gain. In my tradition of faith, little value is placed on visiting holy sites as a way of gaining merit or encountering holiness—and I was troubled by the crowds, competition and control that seemed such a part of those supposed holy places.

But as we continued to visit the different sites around the city and I continued to reflect on the questions they raised, I came to realise we were in Israel not to visit holy places but to rediscover holy stories. These were the stories I had grown up with, that I had learned and even studied at times, and they had become some of the most dominant and most repeated stories in my life.

Visiting Israel was one way to re-engage, to re-imagine, to go deeper into those stories. We saw the places in which they happened—or the possible sites at which they happened. We saw the hills, the lake, the desert wilderness, the city that were the locations for these stories. We heard the people, some of the languages, the bird calls, the wind that would have been their background. And in our group, we re-told the stories again. For me, those holy stories are different in their re-reading and our re-telling because of those experiences.[1]

The movement of people who followed Jesus began with an event—something happened that seemed to change everything, for them and for the world—but it grew through this kind of storytelling. Those who had been with Jesus told the stories of what they had seen and heard and felt. These stories were told and re-told, until a decade or two later some of those who were there began to write down their memories and experiences.

Those who undertook this formal re-telling of the stories of Jesus had to be selective and shape their storytelling to different degrees and in different ways for the purposes for which they were writing. Reflecting on this at the end of his later version of the story, perhaps using some hyperbole, John's gospel concluded, "Jesus also did many other things. If they were all written down, I suppose the whole world could not contain the books that would be written" (John 21:25).

Others talked to people who had been there, collecting some of the stories from those first disciples and other key participants in the story. Perhaps addressing his patron or giving a generic greeting to any who was a "lover of God" as the name Theophilus suggests, Luke acknowledged that he was not the first to undertake this task and not an original witness to what had happened. He explained his methods of historical research and storytelling in this way:

> Many people have set out to write accounts about the events that have been fulfilled among us. They used the eyewitness reports circulating among us from the early disciples. Having carefully investigated everything from the beginning, I also have decided to write an accurate account for you, most honourable Theophilus, so you can be certain of the truth of everything you were taught (Luke 1:1–4).

"Having carefully investigated everything from the beginning, I also have decided to write an accurate account ... so you can be certain of the truth of everything you were taught."

Not only was Luke explaining his process, he was urging its importance and the value of telling the story again, even when we know how the story goes and how it ends. The best stories are not told only once, but we go back to them again and again. We might enjoy them differently, and they also challenge and shape us in different ways at different points in our lives and experiences. The best stories are those that continue to speak to us and our world: "a community of hope has texts that always 'mean' afresh."[2]

Stories matter. They are core to what makes us human. The stories we hear and embrace as youngsters, that we re-tell at family gatherings and in popular culture, that we tell to ourselves can define and shape and change us. This is why hearing a new story can be so exciting and demanding. This is why hearing an old story again can be so comforting and encouraging.

This is why the first argument for faith, hope and love is not an argument, it's this story—the story of Jesus and His birth. And this is why it's important to insist on re-telling this story year after year. It is also why particular occasions and seasons for doing so are such a valuable part of our faith traditions.

Few of us are privileged to visit Bethlehem or Nazareth, the Sea of Galilee or Jerusalem, but the stories that came from those places are available to us all. They are not about holy places to be fought over but holy stories to be told and re-told, enjoyed and celebrated, wrestled with and entered into.

So as we tell the story of the birth of Jesus again this year, let's tell it in the way of God, as so consistent with and representative of who He is. Let's re-tell it with all the beauty, kindness, generosity and goodness we can employ. Let's re-tell it in surprising, humble and creative ways. Let's re-tell it in our actions, our choices, our compassion and all our lives.

1. I wrote at length on these ideas and narrated a later trip to Jordan, Israel and the Palestinian Territories in *Of Falafels and Following Jesus: Stories from a Journey Through the Holy Land*, <www.FalafelsandFollowingJesus.com>.

2. Walter Brueggemann, *Mandate to Difference*, Westminster John Knox Press, 2007, page 104.

22

Messiah

Among the Hebrew scriptures—known in the Bible as the Old Testament—the book of Daniel is one of the most fascinating. First, its story tells of Daniel being taken into exile after the Babylonian capture of the city of Jerusalem and his rise to become a scholar and a politician in the court of Babylon. He served at least three successive kings, including surviving a change of imperial power when the Medo-Persians invaded. The book is also famous for the children's story of "Daniel in the Lion's Den," at the same time as giving some of the biggest picture, history-of-the-world kind of prophecies to be found in the Bible.

But perhaps the most intriguing aspect of the book of Daniel is how it mixes the personal and the prophetic, the intimate and the panoramic, the faithful and the political. Daniel 9 offers a specific glimpse of this. As an old man, Daniel had served in Babylon for many years, but his heart was still distressed about the destruction and continuing desolation of his homeland. In his sadness, he turned to God in prayer, pleading on behalf of his broken nation (see Daniel 9:1–19). "O my God, lean down and listen to me," Daniel prayed. "Open your eyes and see our despair. See how your city—the city that bears your name—lies in ruins. We make this plea, not because we deserve help, but because of your mercy" (Daniel 9:18).

As Daniel continued to pray, the angel Gabriel came to him. About five centuries before he would make his dramatic announcements to Zechariah and Mary, he assured Daniel that Jerusalem would be rebuilt. He delivered a specific prophecy of a time period totalling 70 "sets of seven"—often understood as representing 490 years—beginning at the time of the order to rebuild Jerusalem. Near the end of the time period, Daniel was told, "a ruler—the Anointed One—comes" (Daniel 9:25). The Hebrew term for Anointed One was *Messiah*.

Historically, this prophecy has been used by many scholars and preachers to "prove" the identity and veracity of Jesus as the promised Messiah. Famously, in his commentary on the Bible's prophetic books of Daniel and Revelation, mathematician Sir Isaac Newton described these verses as "the foundation stone of the Christian religion".

While the mathematics connected with this have affirmed the faith of many believers, there might be more to these numbers than simple historical calculations. In the Bible, there are recurring time periods of sevens: Sabbath every seventh day; a sabbatical year every seventh year; and a jubilee at the end of every seven sets of seven years (see Leviticus 25). These were detailed as significant resets for the social, political and economic systems of the Israelite nation. In years of jubilee, land would be returned to its original owners and families, debts were to be forgiven and slaves—those who had fallen into debt—would be set free.

Various Bible scholars have recognised an echo—even a fulfilment—of this jubilee principle in the time period detailed in Daniel 9:

> The jubilee is a fascinating social innovation within the legislation of ancient Israel, a sign that relentless buying and selling of land, goods and even people won't be the last word. But seventy times seven? That sounds like the jubilee of jubilees! So, though 490 years—nearly half a millennium—is indeed a long time, the point is this: when the time finally arrives, it will be the greatest "redemption" of all. This will be the time of real, utter and lasting freedom. That is the hope that sustained the

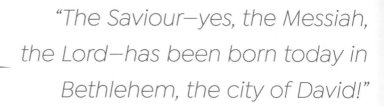

*"The Saviour—yes, the Messiah,
the Lord—has been born today in
Bethlehem, the city of David!"*

Israelites in the long years of the centuries before the time of Jesus.[1]

This was a key element of the anticipation among the people of the Jewish nation at the time when Jesus was born. It is significant to note that Herod's response to the magi's questions about the newborn "king of the Jews" was to ask the religious leaders, "Where is the Messiah supposed to be born?" (Matthew 2:4). Whomever the magi were searching for, this was what and who Israel was expecting.

But this was not only a human assumption. This was the core announcement of the angel to the shepherds outside Bethlehem: "I bring you good news that will bring great joy to all people. The Saviour—yes, the Messiah, the Lord—has been born today in Bethlehem, the city of David!" (Luke 2:10, 11).

We also see another specific and spiritually directed reference to this identity of Jesus in the recognition of the Baby by Simeon when Jesus' parents brought Him to the temple. Simeon was described as someone who "was righteous and devout and was eagerly waiting for the Messiah to come and rescue Israel. The Holy Spirit was upon him and had revealed to him that he would not die until he had seen the Lord's Messiah" (Luke 2:25, 26). Again, the story provides another voice urging that this was happening among them.

Through the gospel stories, *Messiah*—or its Greek equivalent, *Christ*—would be a recurring theme, question and claim. It was the affirmation of His disciples: "We have found the Messiah" (John 1:41). It was the breathless question of the crowds who heard Him teach and saw Him heal: "Could it be that Jesus is the Son of David, the Messiah?" (Matthew 12:23). It was a claim that Jesus made about Himself: "I am the Messiah" (John 4:26).

The *Christ* in "Jesus Christ"—and in *Christ*mas—was not His surname. It was a title that claimed that Jesus was the fulfilment of all the hopes of Israel and all the promises of God to His people. He was the ultimate answer to the earnest prayer of the old, tired and grieving Daniel, who had remained faithful to God over a lifetime of exile, even as his nation remained in ruins. It was the language Jesus used in His first public sermon in His hometown of Nazareth, announcing good news to the poor, freedom for the captives and the oppressed, "and that the time of the Lord's favour has come" (Luke 4:18, 19). It was the beginning of a new hope, the great jubilee, and the restoration and liberation of all humanity.

1. N T Wright, *How God Became King: The Forgotten Story of the Gospels*, HarperCollins, 2012, page 70.

23

Saviour

J oseph often seems the forgotten hero in the story of the birth of Jesus. Yes, he's there in all the nativity scenes, but he is very much a support character. In many re-tellings of the story, he is only a mention along the way. But we should not forget that God was also at work in his life, which was made obvious by angels appearing to him at least three times in Matthew's telling of the story.

The gospels tell us little about Joseph. While Mary reappeared throughout the gospel stories, Joseph was not heard of after their visit to the temple when Jesus was 12 years old (see Luke 2:41–52) and tradition suggests that he probably died some time before Jesus began His public ministry. Later in the story, the people of Nazareth give us a hint of Joseph's profession when they expressed doubts about Jesus' identity. They referred to Jesus as "just the carpenter's son" (Matthew 13:55), with the original language suggesting a craftsman who worked with wood and stone. However, Matthew introduced Joseph with one of the Bible's best descriptors: "a righteous man" (Matthew 1:19).

At the time of Mary's unexpected and unexplainable pregnancy, she was engaged to Joseph. While their culture around engagement was different to how it is usually understood today, the story was clear that their marriage process had not been concluded. Unsurprisingly, Joseph was upset and probably wished to avoid dishonour himself, but he also did not want to publicly shame Mary, choosing to try to protect her from the accusations, gossip and even possible threats to her life that would have been directed at Mary in such a scandalous situation.

But God intervened: "As he considered this, an angel of the Lord appeared to him in a dream. 'Joseph, son of David,' the angel said, 'do not be afraid to take Mary as your wife. For the child within her was conceived by the Holy Spirit'" (Matthew 1:20). Not only did the angel reassure Joseph, giving him a way forward in this difficult situation, he also was given—reinstated to—the father's cultural role of naming the child. The angel continued, "And she will have a son, and you are to name him Jesus, for he will save his people from their sins" (Matthew 1:21).

Naming a child seems a heavy responsibility. But Joseph was given the name and its meaning, and the privilege of being the one to announce it to anyone who was listening in their families, in Bethlehem and Nazareth, and in the wider world. The name probably sounded different on the night He was born though. As a contemporary guide to baby names puts it, "The name Jesus means *God Is Salvation* and . . . is the Greek form of the Hebrew name Yeshu'a, which also gives us the modern name Joshua."[1]

And, of course, this was not merely a name chosen from family tradition or for how it sounds. It was an announcement of who this Baby was and what He would do in the world. Significantly, this was the first title given in the angel's announcement that Jesus had been born: "I bring you good news that will bring great joy to all people. The *Saviour*—yes, the Messiah, the Lord—has been born today in Bethlehem, the city of David!" (Luke 2:10, 11).

This designation of Jesus as Saviour is another echo of His divinity, drawn from the songs of the book of Psalms and the best hopes of the Hebrew prophets. But it was also a specific role in our world and its history. A saviour is someone who gets another person out of trouble, a rescuer, deliverer or protector. And there was truth to this in the ministry Jesus would do, in His healing and teaching. But Jesus was specifically described as One who would "save his people from their sins."

"And she will have a son, and you are to name him Jesus, for he will save his people from their sins."

In the history of the Hebrew people, their sin, their unfaithfulness and the broken relationship between the people and their God went all the way back to the earliest stories of Adam and Eve in a good and perfect world that went wrong because of their selfish and destructive choices. At the time of this earliest sin, there was a promise given of a Child who would crush evil and break its power, begin to set wrongs right and restore the relationships that had been so badly damaged, particularly between humanity and its Creator (see Genesis 3:15).

But, while Jesus was a Jew and His story is best understood in the context of the Jewish scriptures, history and heritage, the angels were adamant that His birth was good news "to all people" (Luke 2:10). Simeon also urged the universal significance of this Child: "I have seen your salvation, which you have prepared for all people" (Luke 2:30, 31). These declarations surrounding the story of the birth of Jesus insisted that Jesus was not only the Jewish Messiah, but the Saviour of all people.

It's the bad news and the good news in one announcement: all humanity needs a saviour—we are all equally broken—and to all humanity, a Saviour has come. As such, the recognition of Jesus as Saviour has become an acknowledgment of our common humanity and human condition. It is also a catalyst for the work of healing broken relationships with each other—across the various human divides, including language, nation, tribe and race—and with the rest of creation.

As "a righteous man", Joseph was entrusted with naming the Saviour and with His early care, including leading their escape into Egypt and their cautious return to Nazareth (see Matthew 2:13–23). His willingness to trust God and follow His leading and to believe Mary's incredible story about her unusual pregnancy were vital contributions to the story of Jesus' birth.

While Joseph the carpenter might have been less likely to burst into poetic and prophetic song than Zechariah the priest, it seems both new fathers would have shared the sentiments and enthusiasm of Zechariah's song:

> Praise the Lord, the God of Israel,
> because he has visited and redeemed his people.
> He has sent us a mighty Saviour
> from the royal line of his servant David,
> just as he promised
> through his holy prophets long ago (Luke 1:68–70).

1. <www.babynames.com>.

24

Glory

Today, Bethlehem is a town of about 50,000 people, with narrow streets winding up, down and around the small Judean hills. One of the places that many of the tourist buses grind their way towards on the edge of town is known as the Shepherds' Field. It's a sparse, rock-strewn park with a few low trees and some patchy gardening and, across the road, a string of shops specialising in souvenirs carved from olive wood.

A small, pale-stoned Franciscan church sits in the middle of the park. There is also a fountain splashing water over a stone sculpture of a shepherd and his sheep, as well as a series of caves that have been converted into intimate chapels. These chapels, adorned with miniature nativity scenes and with their ceilings blackened by the smoke of countless candles, are places that many of the busloads of visitors file into for a short time of worship. They invariably sing a Christmas carol or two from their own tradition of faith and in their own language. It is a place in which it always sounds like Christmas.

Towards the back of the park, near the edge of the low hill on which it sits, a number of shaded outdoor chapel spaces look over a dry valley to the surrounding hills. The hillsides are rocky, with small tufts of beige grass and clumps of the darker greens of olive trees or small pine trees. Shepherds and their sheep have often been seen making their way along this valley, even in recent years, although this is becoming less common as the continuing spread of the town and surrounding settlements push the shepherds and their flocks further away.

It's a remarkable place to pause, to sit and reflect, to remember and imagine the story that happened on these hills. As you listen to the sound of the breeze gently hissing through the pine needles and feel the dry dustiness of the air, you can almost hear the murmurs of a group of men on a quiet evening and imagine the sounds and smell of the sheep: "That night there were shepherds staying in the fields nearby, guarding their flocks of sheep. Suddenly, an angel of the Lord appeared among them, and the radiance of the Lord's glory surrounded them" (Luke 2:8, 9).

The first thing we tend to think of when we hear *glory* in a context like this is some kind of really bright light. It seems this was part of the experience of these startled shepherds. It would have been dark out on those hills as they settled in for the night, with only a small fire at best.

The appearance of this heavenly being would have split the darkness and Luke's description used the language of light, but it seems that this was more than a bright light. It was more like a wonderful presence that surrounded them. In the cool of the night, the shepherds might have felt its warmth and even some kind of profound emotion, far deeper than their initial alarm.

By the presence of this angel, the shepherds were somehow drawn into the glory of God.

The angel delivered the good news of Jesus' birth and gave instructions about where to find the Baby, then the focus shifted again: "Suddenly, the angel was joined by a vast host of others—the armies of heaven—praising God and saying, 'Glory to God in highest heaven, and peace on earth to those with whom God is pleased'" (Luke 2:13, 14). It seems obvious that the song of the angels was not describing or ascribing to God mere brightness, as overwhelming as that might be. This declaration of glory was an exaltation of His greatness and goodness, the quality of His character and the wonder of His actions, a splendour that was so much more than appearance.

These two related uses of *glory* occur repeatedly throughout the Bible. It becomes a shorthand for God's appearance and presence,

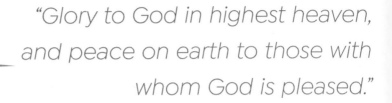

"Glory to God in highest heaven, and peace on earth to those with whom God is pleased."

as well as His greatness of magnitude and nature. As in the case of the shepherds, glory can be wonderful and terrifying at the same time. And it seems to be both a literal, physical reality and a metaphor that represents so much more. From the perspective of human experience, it seems "glory is what God looks like when for the time being all you have to look at Him with is a pair of eyes."[1]

Sitting looking over the bare hills and the encroaching housing developments on the outskirts of Bethlehem, it seemed to me an unlikely place for such a display of God's glory. But the appearance of glory amid the seemingly mundane is so much a part of the wonder and transformation to be found in the story of Jesus' birth. The story also urges that the greater glory was not the dazzling appearance of the angels, the overwhelming experience of the shepherds or even the vast host of angels singing their hearts out in praise of God and His astonishing goodness. The greatest glory was Jesus Himself.

Those who told the stories of Jesus insisted that the most tangible way to encounter the glory of God in our world was Jesus, as unlikely as it might have seemed. In a letter to the second generation of believers in the story of Jesus, John emphasised both the physical reality of their experience with Jesus and its ultimate transcendence:

We proclaim to you the one who existed from the beginning, whom we have heard and seen. We saw him with our own eyes and touched him with our own hands. He is the Word of life. This one who is life itself was revealed to us, and we have seen him. And now we testify and proclaim to you that he is the one who is eternal life. He was with the Father, and then he was revealed to us (1 John 1:1, 2).

One aspect of the incarnation is that God hid and even put aside His glory in becoming Jesus, to be born as a baby—but, in a greater sense, in this action and this story, His glory shines all the brighter.

---

1. Frederick Buechner, *Wishful Thinking: A Seeker's ABC* (Revised and Expanded), HarperSanFrancisco, 1993, page 35.

25

Something happened.

Something happened that was so significant that every year we pause and sing songs about it, share gifts with each other and re-tell the story.

Something happened that so transformed the world that we are still celebrating it more than 2000 years later, even while the larger project is so obviously incomplete.

Something happened that was so marvellous that even the first participants seemed unable to contain themselves and songs kept bursting out of them.

Something began that was the most serious thing in the history of our world—and it was overflowing with joy.

Joy was part of the key announcements of the babies to be born and the event that was to happen. For Zechariah, joy was to be his and Elizabeth's but would also echo in the wider world: "You will have great joy and gladness, and many will rejoice at his birth," said the angel (Luke 1:14). When Mary visited Elizabeth, the joy was personal and physical: "When I heard your greeting, the baby in my womb jumped for joy" (Luke 1:44). And the angel who announced Jesus' birth to the shepherds calmed their individual fears but promised that what he was about to tell them was cause for global celebration: "'Don't be afraid!' he said. 'I bring you good news that will bring great joy to all people'" (Luke 2:10). Joy was the direct consequence and the exclamation mark on each of these announcements.

With all these celebrations, anticipations and promises of joy, it seems hardly surprising that the story of the birth of Jesus was also seasoned with songs. Understanding the announcements of what was to come, Mary and Zechariah—as soon as he could again speak—sang songs of praise and wonder and prophecy at what God was doing for them, for His people and for the world. Of course, the vast host of angels also sang to their small and unlikely audience in the fields outside Bethlehem.

But the angels' joy was contagious, shared by those who encountered and recognised the Baby. After they had followed the angel's directions to the manger, "the shepherds went back to their flocks, glorifying and praising God for all they had heard and seen. It was just as the angel had told them" (Luke 2:20). Similarly, Simeon and Anna each praised God when they encountered the baby Jesus in the temple. In Matthew's telling of the story, the magi also celebrated when they finally arrived in Bethlehem and realised that they had reached the end of their quest: "When they saw the star, they were filled with joy!" (Matthew 2:10). None of these people were otherwise connected to this specific family or particular birth, but somehow they knew that the most appropriate response was joy.

This was not merely the joy of the happy news of a newborn baby, as joyous as such an event can be. Each of these announcements, songs and responses emphasised something larger happening in the world. This was not only a new baby, it was a new beginning. In this story, "we know about the God who transforms, makes new and begins again. No wonder creation and humanity, one at a time, all together, sing of the new world bursting with the abundant glory of God."[1]

Yet perhaps this was even more than something that happened, as good, wonderful, glorious and joyous as that something might be. More than this it seems that, in the story of the birth of Jesus, what these various participants and witnesses experienced was something of heaven spilling over into our world. This was not merely an

"The shepherds went back to their flocks, glorifying and praising God for all they had heard and seen. It was just as the angel had told them."

event of human history, as central and pivotal as it was in that context, it was an intersection between two realms of existence.

The trajectory of the big stories of the Bible is of God coming to earth, to humanity. The Bible describes God bending down to form the first human being from the dust of our world and breathing life into him (see Genesis 2:7). Then, in the garden, after their sin, God came to Adam and Eve to spend time with them and to search for them, calling out with the evening breeze, "Where are you?" (Genesis 3:9).

When God freed the Israelites from slavery and established them as a new nation, He asked the people to build a place where He could be: "I will live among the people of Israel and be their God" (Exodus 29:45). Throughout the history of the Israelite nation, speaking through prophets and leaders, God repeatedly called out to the people to assure them of His enduring love and His desire to be with them. The movement of God was always towards humanity, bringing heaven to earth.

Jesus would even teach His followers to pray: "May your Kingdom come. . . . May your will be done on earth, as it is in heaven" (Matthew 6:10). But, in the birth of Jesus, the realm of heaven and the reign of God had already come to earth in a new and tangible way: "So the Word became human and made his home among us" (John 1:14). Heaven was now here.

And with it—with Him—came joy.

If we take this story seriously, joy was inevitable and uncontainable. As C S Lewis famously put it, "joy is the serious business of heaven."[2] Joy had come into our world in a new and tangible way.

As we re-tell the story again, if it is not a story of joy, we are not telling it aright. The story of Jesus' birth included its human share of fear, uncertainty, oppression, poverty and grief. But real joy was not dependent on or dimmed by such circumstances. While our world continues to suffer in so many of these ways and more, in Jesus, "his life brought light to everyone . . . [and] the light shines in the darkness" (John 1:4, 5). Joy is not only possible, it is anticipated.

Re-telling the story of the birth of Jesus must mean celebration and joy. We re-tell the story—John would write later—"so that you may fully share our joy" (1 John 1:4).

Something happened so full of joy that we still celebrate Him, still sing songs about Him, still re-tell His story, still share our joy.

Jesus happened.

1. Walter Brueggemann, *Celebrating Abundance: Devotions for Advent*, Westminster John Knox Press, 2017, page 17.

2. C S Lewis, *Prayer: Letters to Malcolm*, Fount, 1998, page 90.

26

Horror

In December, 2012, I had been booked to speak at a church on the weekend before Christmas—eight days after the mass murder of 26 people, including 20 six- and seven-year-old children at the Sandy Hook Elementary School. Like many others who were writing and delivering "Christmas messages" over the 10 days following that horrific event, the usual sweet Christmas stories and nativity scenes seemed inadequate to me. Yet a darker and less told—for obvious reasons—part of the story seemed to have a grim resonance.

The event took place in the aftermath of the visit of the magi as a result of Herod's continuing paranoia at the possibility of a new king being born in Israel. Herod had instructed these visitors to report back to him about what they might have discovered in Bethlehem, but "God had warned them in a dream not to return to Herod" (Matthew 2:12), so they slipped away from Jerusalem and out of the story.

Not long after, another dream awoke Joseph with instructions to escape from Bethlehem to Egypt. Realising the magi had ignored his request, Herod had decided to solve the potential problem in his characteristic way: "He sent soldiers to kill all the boys in and around Bethlehem who were two years old and under, based on the wise men's report of the star's first appearance" (Matthew 2:16).

Estimates from archaeologists and historians suggest that there were between 300 to 1000 residents of Bethlehem at the time of Jesus' birth. The demographics of a population of that size would suggest that there might have been between seven and 20 baby boys in the age group targeted by Herod. That this mass killing was not recorded in the history books of the time suggests that such "small" outrages were not unusual during the reign of Herod. But, of course, this was not a small tragedy for the families and this small community.

Matthew did not describe the murder and the mayhem of that night, which so contrasts with the usual sentiments that surround the story of the birth of Jesus. Instead, he quoted a lament from the writings of the Hebrew prophet Jeremiah, which seemed to point directly to this moment, with its reference to the region of Ramah and Rachel, the wife of the Hebrew patriarch Isaac, who was buried nearby:

A cry was heard in Ramah—
weeping and great mourning.
Rachel weeps for her children,
refusing to be comforted,
for they are dead (Matthew 2:18).

Reflecting on this story and this lament in the wake of the Sandy Hook massacre, it bothered me that these verses were the last we hear of the little town of Bethlehem in the Bible story. Bethlehem had been an important town in the history of Israel. It was where Ruth made her home, where David was born, and it kept appearing in these stories. But then we were left with this unanswered expression of grief—and we simply fade to black on Bethlehem.

It also bothered me that the gospels did not record any instances of Jesus re-visiting the town of His birth. As we have noted, Bethlehem is only a short distance from Jerusalem, so according to the gospels' stories, Jesus was in the area a number of times during His three years of public ministry. It doesn't seem like He could have ignored this part of His story and the impact it had on this village.

So as one way of wrestling with the news headlines and the questions that inevitably come with such outrages, I imagined and wrote a story—what might have been if we had a record of Jesus

*"God blesses those who mourn,
for they will be comforted."*

visiting Bethlehem on the 30th anniversary of this tragedy and finally comforting a mother named Rachel, whose baby boy had been murdered on that horrific long-ago night. I simply told that story as the Christmas "sermon" in the church I was visiting that year.[1]

In the aftermath of the Sandy Hook school shooting, questions about "Why?" and "Where was God?" were fresh and raw—especially so, given that children were so brutally targeted. But they were not always answered helpfully by some of the louder Christian voices.

The story of the "Massacre of the Innocents"—as it has come to be called in Christian history—offers a different perspective on these questions. It was a bitter irony that the tragedy that had visited Bethlehem was not because of the people's godlessness, as some would have undoubtedly alleged, or because of God's indifferent absence, as so many more would have argued by their desperate and grief-stricken "Where was God?" questions. Instead, this horrific crime came about precisely because of His presence.

This was a reality that we noted previously in the unusual Christmas story of Revelation. A great dragon "stood in front of the woman as she was about to give birth, ready to devour her baby as soon as it was born" (Revelation 12:4). Foiled in this plot, the dragon refused to admit defeat and broadened his murderous intent: "And the dragon was angry at the woman and declared war against the rest of her children" (Revelation 12:17). The baby boys of Bethlehem and the children of Sandy Hook were victims of this dragon. In this great war, Evil hurts God through hurting His children.

But God is not remote from this suffering and grief. While Jesus was able to escape from the dragon's attack, fleeing with Joseph and Mary as refugees to Egypt for a time, the story of Jesus is located in the reality of the sorrows of our world. Immanuel—"God is with us" (Matthew 1:23)—was not merely a name, it was the identification and co-suffering of Jesus in the tragedies of our lives and our world, not least of which would be His own cruel and unjust death. We don't have answers to many of our questions, but "God is with us" speaks to those parents—and all of us—who feel those painful anniversaries that accumulate in all our lives.

At the heart of my imagined story was what I believe about Jesus and, through Him, what God is like. He could not have ignored the grief of Bethlehem. He was with us in all the experiences of our world and He is with us in our darkest days, those times in which we refuse to be comforted. He cares—and somehow He and His story comfort us.

As Jesus would teach, "God blesses those who mourn, for they will be comforted" (Matthew 5:4).

---

1. Read this story "After 30 Years" at <www.signspublishing.com.au/Advent>.

27

Teaching

In traditionally Christian cultures, many of the teachings of Jesus have become clichés. We often hear people talk about "going the extra mile," "turning the other cheek" or "casting pearls before swine". We might joke about how the "last shall be first" or describe someone as "the salt of the earth" or acting as a "good Samaritan" to us or to someone else. Clichés are expressions that have become almost meaningless by their overuse, belying the fact that they have been used so often because of the meaning they once carried. While they are now used almost unthinkingly, they once caught our collective cultural attention because of the aptness or freshness of their expression.

So one of the challenges we have is to hear the teaching of Jesus anew. Part of this challenge is that because a few of these clichés are familiar to us, we can think we know Jesus and what He taught. This might lead us to reject further information about Him before it can be considered: "In His case, quite frankly, presumed familiarity has led to unfamiliarity, unfamiliarity has led to contempt and contempt has led to profound ignorance."[1] Many of us do not know Jesus or about Jesus as much as we think we do.

The first and most important step for re-hearing Jesus today is to reconsider the realities, stories and claims that surrounded Jesus' birth—who He was and why His coming into the world was so significant. We have reflected on many aspects of these stories and it should not surprise us that what Jesus taught sounds likes the claims and values embodied in these stories. As such, the declarations made about Jesus—and that He made about Himself—do not allow us to categorise Him as merely another great teacher or wise guru, humanitarian or all-round nice guy.

Jesus understood and insisted that He was God in the world. "Anyone who has seen me has seen the Father!" He would tell His first disciples (John 14:9). This was seen, heard and experienced in who He was, how He interacted with people throughout His life, in His death and resurrection—and in His teaching. Indeed, for many of those who came to follow Jesus, His teaching would have been their first and possibly primary exposure to who He was. A number of times the gospels recorded the questions and amazement of the people who heard Him speak: "When Jesus had finished saying these things, the crowds were amazed at his teaching, for he taught with real authority—quite unlike their teachers of religious law" (Matthew 7:28, 29).

It's intriguing to recognise that Jesus' teaching was also noticeably different from what is often taught in many churches today. Jesus usually didn't teach doctrine or theology in a way that fits modern-day formulations. Rather, Jesus told stories that invited people into the alternative living reality of the kingdom of God. When He gave commands, they most often related to how to resist the pressures of a violent, unjust, inauthentic and uncertain world, and to live and love well with both personal faithfulness and public action. In short, "the way of discipleship [what it means to follow Jesus] and the commands of Jesus are most explicitly taught in the Sermon on the Mount."[2]

Church historians urge that the Sermon on the Mount (see Matthew 5–7) was the most referenced biblical passage in the first 300 years of the church: "This was the main way the early Christians were taught how to be disciples."[3] But the ethical teachings of Jesus seemed to fall out of favour and then almost out of sight as the church changed, becoming more focused on form, theology and doctrines, as well as politics and power structures. What Jesus taught became increasingly uncomfortable in the context of what the church had become.

"When Jesus had finished saying these things, the crowds were amazed at his teaching, for he taught with real authority—quite unlike their teachers of religious law."

Consider, for example, Jesus' ethic for the worst-case scenario in human relationships—the command to "love your enemies! Pray for those who persecute you!" (Matthew 5:44). While humanity is always seeking to define who is in and out, who we should fear and hate, Jesus commanded His disciples to love, even when "they" actually do seek our harm. And love is not merely contriving nice feelings towards "them" but actively seeking the enemy's good, even at cost to ourselves. We do this best when we are not worrying about the stuff of our own lives (see Matthew 6:25).

Not only was this counter-intuitive and counter-cultural in Jesus' day, it has been ever since and remains so today. If we take Jesus' teachings seriously, they will change not only our personal relationships and priorities but our public engagement—how we listen and speak, how we vote and advocate, and how we seek to include and welcome people who are different into our lives and communities.

Contradicting many of our assumptions about faith and spirituality, the teachings of Jesus were remarkably practical. Teaching His disciples to pray, Jesus focused on the reality of the kingdom of God, that God's will be done on earth, and that our physical needs are met, our relationships are healed and that we are protected from the evil in our world (see Matthew 6:9–13). Rather than an abstract or disengaged holiness, Jesus taught a lived faithfulness. We enter into the realities of the kingdom of God by practising His teaching, meaning that we do it and then we do it again and again. We are transformed by God's presence in our lives, our growing partnership with Him and by living in His ways.

The teachings of Jesus—as summarised in the Sermon on the Mount—are the rock on which His disciples were called to build their faith and their lives (see Matthew 7:24). Based on the stories of Jesus and the claims about who He was, to seek to live this out today means a life that resists what is wrong around us and in us, that loves well even when it costs, that seeks first the reality and priorities of the kingdom of God (see Matthew 6:33). So much more than any clichés or spiritual assumptions, it's a life worth continuing to discover and to teach, worth inviting others to share.

1. Dallas Willard, *The Divine Conspiracy*, Fount, 1998, page 1.

2. David P Gushee and Glen H Stassen, *Kingdom Ethics: Following Jesus in Contemporary Context* (Second Edition), Eerdmans Publishing Co, 2016, page 89.

3. ibid.

28

Death

God was dead.

The claim that "God is dead" has been a refrain with continuing appeal to many. While the cry was popularised by the philosopher Friedrich Nietzsche more than a century ago, many philosophers and scientists continue to argue against the existence of God. If God was ever needed to explain the world, they argue, we don't need Him anymore—so God is dead.

Many Christian theologians, preachers and writers have spent a lot of time arguing back. But Nietzsche and his followers were right— once. Just once in the history of our world, this statement was true. On that dark Friday afternoon at the other end of Jesus' life, the crowd "went home in deep sorrow" and Jesus' friends "stood at a distance watching" (Luke 23:48, 49). They could truly and literally have mumbled to each other in stunned astonishment, grief and despair, "God is dead."

As the stories of the gospels tell it, God was dead. In Jesus, God became human, experienced our brokenness, and suffered a grisly and very human death. He was literally and completely dead. The apostle Paul's hymn of the incarnation and humility of Jesus saw this as a further step of humiliation: "When he appeared in human form, he humbled himself in obedience to God and died a criminal's death on a cross" (Philippians 2:7, 8).

In *The Idiot*, Russian writer Fyodor Dostoyevsky confronts one of his characters with a painting showing Christ just after He was taken from the cross. It was a description based on Dostoyevsky's own experience of seeing—and being deeply moved by—Hans Holbein the Younger's painting, "Dead Christ," in a museum in Basel, Switzerland, in 1867:

> I think that painters have usually been in the habit of depicting Christ, both on the cross and when taken down from it, still with a nuance of extraordinary beauty in the face; this beauty they seek to preserve in him even during his most terrible torments. But in [this] painting there was no trace of beauty; this really was the corpse of a man who had endured endless torments.[1]

The description reflects on the questions raised by such a picture, particularly how a Person who had raised the dead in the course of His ministry had been so implacably reduced and destroyed by the horror of death. God was dead.

Dostoyevsky's contemplation extends to the people, outside the frame of the painting, who had witnessed this death and "must have felt a terrible anguish and perturbation that evening, which had smashed all their hopes and almost all their beliefs in one go."[2] Death always brings shattering and shuddering, but the death of God was so much more—world-shattering, universe-shuddering but somehow also world-changing and world-redeeming.

Like so much of the incarnation of Jesus and the unanswered—perhaps unanswerable—questions that surround the stories of His birth and His life, we don't understand everything about how the death of Jesus changed the relationship between God and humanity or how it offers "everyone who believes in him . . . eternal life" (John 3:16). The Bible describes how the sin of the first human beings broke this relationship, as well the relationships we have with each other and the rest of creation. We have noted this pattern of God coming to humanity to seek to restore that relationship and that ultimately this was fulfilled in Jesus.

Right from the first promise given to Adam and Eve, it was anticipated that this project of restoring humanity and defeating evil

"So now we can rejoice in our wonderful new relationship with God because our Lord Jesus Christ has made us friends of God."

would cost God some kind of injury (see Genesis 3:15). Often performed in the Christmas season, Handel's *Messiah* spends less time focusing on the stories of Jesus' birth than it does on giving attention to the Hebrew prophecies of the coming One who would suffer for the sin of the people. It draws on texts such as those in Isaiah 53:

> Unjustly condemned, he was led away. No-one cared that he died without descendants, that his life was cut short in midstream. But he was struck down for the rebellion of my people. He had done no wrong and had never deceived anyone. But he was buried like a criminal; he was put in a rich man's grave. . . . And because of his experience, my righteous servant will make it possible for many to be counted righteous, for he will bear all their sins (Isaiah 53:8–11).

As the angel told Joseph, Jesus was named as the One who "will save his people from their sins" (Matthew 1:21). Yet among theologians, scholars and preachers, there are various theories of atonement, as such studies are known. Many point to the model of the Hebrew sacrificial system in which an innocent animal would be sacrificed for the forgiveness and removal of sins; others to how, in Jesus, God non-violently endured the worst of evil and so exposed and overcame that evil; other Christian traditions emphasise the resurrection as the defeat of evil, sin and death.

It is a many-faceted story. Our human language and metaphors come up short and can lead us to wrong conclusions if we push them too far in describing this indescribable gift (see 2 Corinthians 9:15). But it seems obvious from the story that this was planned and that somehow the cruel and unjust death of Jesus became "good news to all people"—individually and collectively:

> But God showed his great love for us by sending Christ to die for us while we were still sinners. And since we have been made right in God's sight by the blood of Christ, he will certainly save us from God's condemnation. For since our friendship with God was restored by the death of his Son while we were still his enemies, we will certainly be saved through the life of his Son (Romans 5:8–10).

Author Douglas Coupland was once asked his greatest fear. He replied: "That God exists, but doesn't care very much for humans."[3] In Jesus and His death, God reversed and undid this great fear: God does care, very much, for humans—so much that He was prepared to sacrifice His existence to demonstrate that care and to make possible our eternal restoration, reconnection and relationship with Him. God was dead—"so now we can rejoice in our wonderful new relationship with God because our Lord Jesus Christ has made us friends of God" (Romans 5:11).

1. Fyodor Dostoyevsky, *The Idiot* (Penguin Classics), Penguin Books, 2004, Kindle Edition, page 475.

2. ibid, page 477.

3. Douglas Coupland, "P.S.: About the Author" in *Girlfriend in a Coma*, Harper Perennial, 2004, page 2.

29

Resurrection

As Tolkien put it, "the Birth of Christ is the eucatastrophe [the unexpected turning point for good] of history. The Resurrection is the eucatastrophe of the story of the Incarnation. The story begins and ends in joy."[1] God was dead—and then He was alive again. This was the central miracle of the story of Jesus and the fact that transformed the first followers of Jesus.

After the death of Jesus, it would have been expected that His disciples would have gradually returned to their lives, their homes, their former professions, and any movement among them would have petered out. But something happened. Something the grieving and shattered disciples did not expect and that they struggled to accept. The women rushing breathlessly from the tomb that Sunday morning were "very frightened but also filled with great joy" (Matthew 28:8). Even after the risen Jesus had appeared to His disciples several times, "they worshipped him—but some of them doubted!" (Matthew 28:17). But, with time, reflection and growing faith, they came to understand this as the most remarkable experience of their lives and in the history of our world.

Throughout history, countless people have died—too many of them as victims of horrible and unjust violence—but Jesus' death was transformed by resurrection. It is only the Resurrection that allows us to see victory in His death. Without it, He would have been just another failed Messiah. For all His great teaching, healing and wisdom, He would likely have been forgotten long ago. It is only because of His resurrection that we remember His birth.

Indeed, it is unlikely that the New Testament would exist, except for the fact that—as Luke would describe Jesus' parting commands to His disciples—"You are witnesses of all these things" (Luke 24:48). Luke would begin his second book and history of the early church—the book of Acts—with this same theme: "During the forty days after he suffered and died, he appeared to the apostles from time to time, and he proved to them in many ways that he was actually alive" (Acts 1:3).

Similarly, a later convert to the way of Jesus, writing about 20 years after Jesus' death and resurrection, Paul would document this sequence of events, acknowledging its fulfilment of God's plan and the witnesses of it:

> Christ died for our sins, just as the Scriptures said. He was buried, and he was raised from the dead on the third day, just as the Scriptures said. He was seen by Peter and then by the Twelve. After that, he was seen by more than 500 of his followers at one time, most of whom are still alive, though some have died (1 Corinthians 15:3–6).

The historic reality of the Resurrection—as improbable or impossible as it might seem to us—is the best explanation of the historical evidence that we have and of those who bore witness to it, many of them at the cost of their own lives. It changed frightened fishermen into bold proclaimers of the reign of Jesus. Doubters surrendered their disbelief; sceptics became sure; in Paul's case, a persecutor became a preacher after being confronted with the reality of the resurrected Jesus (see 1 Corinthians 15:8, 9).

Without these experiences, evidences and witnesses, the movement of Jesus that formed into the early church would instead have been over by that first Sunday evening. As Paul would admit, he would not otherwise have had much to preach: "And if Christ has not been raised, then all our preaching is useless, and your faith is useless" (1 Corinthians 15:14). The reality of the Resurrection is the key question on which the significance of Jesus, the kingdom He announced and the things He taught rise or fall. Those who knew

"Christ died for our sins, just as the Scriptures said. He was buried, and he was raised from the dead on the third day, just as the Scriptures said."

Him rose from the seeming defeat of the crucifixion and were convinced that what they had experienced was somehow a glorious new beginning.

But these first believers, particularly those whose writing and preaching are preserved in the New Testament, were adamant that while Jesus' resurrection was unique, "Christ was raised as the first of the harvest" (1 Corinthians 15:23). This means that His resurrection somehow broke the power of death and offered the promise that one day death will come to an end and will even be undone.

As such, the story of Jesus' resurrection gives a powerful perspective for living well as finite and mortal human beings. Death is the ultimate limitation on the capacity of who we can be. And with its apparent finality, it seems to be a negation of everything that is good and right and true and beautiful. If the best of us and everything we do is destined to be dust, what ultimately matters?

Death is also the mechanism of injustice, oppression and suffering in our world. It is the threat behind coercive power and the ultimate end to righteous and courageous resistance. It is hardly surprising that the first generation of Christians would understand death as "the last enemy to be destroyed" (1 Corinthians 15:26). But they also recognised that their allegiance to Jesus would somehow transcend death.

Death had been defeated and so death could be faced boldly when necessary.

This was not an other-worldly spiritual kind of reality. The actual, physical this-worldly resurrection of Jesus affirmed the value, worth and vocation of working for good in our world. Paul summed up his extended dissertation on the reality, hope and implications of the resurrection of Jesus with a call to re-engage with good work in our world, in His name: "So, my dear brothers and sisters, be strong and immovable. Always work enthusiastically for the Lord, for you know that nothing you do for the Lord is ever useless" (1 Corinthians 15:58).

The meaning of the resurrection of Jesus today is that everything matters. Every kindness, every smile, every glimpse of beauty, every gentle moment, every gasp of joy, every embrace, every tear that mourns the loss of something good or someone loved. Everything matters.

And because every little thing matters, every big thing matters too. Every act that changes the world, every choice that affirms life, every voice for justice, every act of creativity and courage, every time we choose love over fear, every time we stand up for what is right and good, every time we seek and celebrate eucatastrophes.

Resurrection is not a case to be made or an argument to be won, so much as it is a story to be told, a life to be lived, a reality to be enacted in our world and a hope to be nurtured. In the name of Jesus, in the light of His resurrection.

1. J R R Tolkien, "On Fairy-Stories" in *Tree and Leaf*, HarperCollins, 2001, page 72.

30

Advent

Hearing the claims about the transformative, transcendent and defining events of Jesus' birth, life, death and resurrection raises some obvious and urgent questions. If the incarnation of Jesus changed everything, why is the world still so broken? If Jesus' birth was the catalyst for a new beginning in the history of our world, why did so much of it seem to continue unabated? If songs are more powerful than decrees, why do decrees still seem to rule the world? If Jesus announced a jubilee, why do injustice and oppression remain so stubborn and persistent? If Jesus' death restored our relationship with God, why do we still feel so estranged from Him and from each other? If Jesus' resurrection marked the defeat of death, why does death still seem to have the last and tragic word in all our stories? If this was good news, why isn't the news better?

These are legitimate and important questions. But the answer of faith is that the story of Jesus—and the place in the story into which we are invited—is incomplete. The project that was inaugurated in our world with the birth of Jesus is yet to be finalised. But the reality of God breaking into the history of our world is the foundation for the expectation that He will do so again.

Traditionally, Advent calendars were about much more than a chocolate a day throughout December. When celebrated thoughtfully, the sense of anticipation of Jesus' "coming" builds over the weeks of the Advent season towardss Christmas, reflecting the expectation that has surrounded faith in God throughout history.

As such, perhaps the most important way to be faithful to the story of Jesus' birth is to continue to expect God—and to expect Him to act in our lives and our world. In the traditional Christian calendar, the Advent season celebrated the stories surrounding the birth of Jesus but also included reflections on and anticipation of God's future acts in history: "Advent is not really the season for preparing for Jesus' birth, as though He had never come in the first place. Advent is the season of preparation for His coming again."[1] The two events are inextricably linked.

It is difficult to embrace the story of Jesus without at least considering His many promises to come again. And the connection between the two events was emphasised by the angels who comforted Jesus' first disciples moments after His post-resurrection departure from earth: "This same Jesus . . . will come back" (Acts 1:11, NIV). By celebrating the reality of Jesus' first coming, we point forward to His return.

Although they seemed stubbornly unable to understand what He was telling them, Jesus had taught His disciples that He would be going away. He warned them that there would be ongoing trouble in the world, including the destruction of the city of Jerusalem and its temple, which took place in 70 AD. He told them bluntly that those who followed Him would be persecuted from time to time, but that God would still be with them (see Luke 21:12–19).

As His return neared, He explained, there would be increasing turmoil and fear in the world, but those who follow Him should take courage: "Then everyone will see the Son of Man coming on a cloud with power and great glory. So when all these things begin to happen, stand and look up, for your salvation is near!" (Luke 21:27, 28).

Across the New Testament, it seems obvious that the first and second generations of disciples expected Jesus to return in their lifetimes—and this has been the expectation of many generations of followers of Jesus who have re-told the stories about Him. But He indicated that "no-one knows the day or hour when these things will

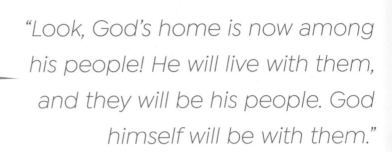

"Look, God's home is now among his people! He will live with them, and they will be his people. God himself will be with them."

happen" (Matthew 24:36), that there would seem to be a delay (see Matthew 25:5), and that His return would take humanity by surprise. Jesus made repeated calls to stay awake and alert (see Luke 21:34–36). While the timing remains uncertain, His return is promised still and remains a joyous hope for those who follow Him.

The Bible describes this second coming of Jesus as the time of resurrection, transformation and judgment. It is best understood as the time of setting wrongs right, undoing the damage and healing the wounds of thousands of years of human history, and the final defeat of the dragon of death (see Revelation 12; 20:7–15). The second coming is less about legal adjudication by a harsh and stern God—remember, this was not the portrayal of God we saw in Jesus (see John 14:9); rather, Jesus' teaching about this time emphasised the choices that each person makes in their lives for or against Jesus Himself and the realities of the kingdom of God (see Matthew 25). The offer in the story of Jesus challenges our acceptance of the inevitability of evil, sin and death, always inviting us to choose goodness, justice and life instead.

Our hearts and minds have been so colonised by these evils that it can be hard to imagine our world re-created, restored and made new—free of death, sorrow and pain. But this is urged as the logical conclusion of the story of the birth of Jesus (see Revelation 21:1–5). At the end of the Bible's story, continuing God's trajectory towards humanity and "God with us," the final movement is that heaven comes down to this planet as a great city, with a loud proclamation: "Look, God's home is now among his people! He will live with them, and they will be his people. God himself will be with them" (Revelation 21:3).

This is the ultimate expression and fulfilment of Advent. We have previously referenced Paul's hymn to the humility of Jesus in stepping down into our world, our humanity and even death on a cross. But this hymn had a second verse, a celebration of the resurrected honour of Jesus, as well as His future glory and reign, a time when all the claims made about Jesus at His birth will be fully and finally completed:

> Therefore, God elevated him to the place of highest
>   honour
> and gave him the name above all other names,
> that at the name of Jesus every knee should bow,
> in heaven and on earth and under the earth,
> and every tongue declare that Jesus Christ is Lord,
> to the glory of God the Father (Philippians 2:9–11).

The story of the birth of Jesus demands a sequel. The promises of the birth of Jesus need fulfilment. His unfinished project and our many questions require resolution. This same Jesus said He will return.

As one of the older traditional Christmas carols put it, "O come, O come, Immanuel!"

---

1. Fleming Rutledge, *Advent: The Once & Future Coming of Jesus*, Eerdmans Publishing Co, 2018, page 76.

31

Hope

Ultimately, the story of the birth of Jesus is good news because it is a story of hope. Describing this event in poetic language, John's gospel asserts that, in Jesus, "the light shines in the darkness, and the darkness can never extinguish it" (John 1:5).

Borrowing from this language can help us understand how hope works. The first step would be to consider the history of Jesus, what He did and who He claimed to be. Although this might seem long ago and far away, at the least this is a point of light by which to navigate on a dark night. From the experiences of the first disciples, John would urge that we can rely on the stories of Jesus as history and a source of ongoing joy (see 1 John 1:1–4, see also Luke 1:4). He would also urge this seemingly small point of light as an entry point for discovering the still greater light and glory in the fullness of God (see John 1:14).

As a second reference point, we can consider what Jesus taught, what the Bible points forward to and what we can believe about what the world ought to be and will be (see Revelation 21:1–5). Expanding on this metaphor of light, John described a future in which there will be no more night "for the glory of God illuminates the city, and the Lamb [symbolic of Jesus] is its light" (Revelation 21:23). This is a light ahead of us, which orients us towards what is of ultimate value and guides the priorities we choose to pursue.

A point behind and a point ahead are basic aids to navigation, particularly points of light amid darkness. But the lights that John described were not static points on distant horizons, rather they were lights that shone into the darkness of our world: "the Word became human" (John 1:14). As we have seen, the trajectory of the history of God and humanity—pre-eminently in the story of the birth of Jesus—is God coming to humanity, the kingdom of God coming into reality in our world. Both the light of the past and the promised light of the future are beams of light that shine to illuminate our today, augmented by the promise that God's presence is always with us (see Matthew 28:20).

This is how hope works. What we believe about the past and what we anticipate about the future change today. And the story of the birth of Jesus offers both a transformed understanding of history and a promise of what our future can be—which makes today different. Which makes us different. Which changes our world and how we live in it.

As we reflected on the context of cosmic conflict into which Jesus was born, we heard a call to be agents of resistance in support of the newborn and rightful King who has come but whose kingdom is yet to be finally realised in our world. This is a call to be agents of hope.

The story of Jesus' birth is a powerful resource for this work. It alerts us to the fact that there is more going on in our world than we can see or understand—and much of it good. So we reject the voices and the assumptions that tell us that what we see and feel are all there is and all that can be. We resist despair or resignation in our choices, actions, engagement and creativity, always seeking to overcome evil by putting our hope into practice, by insisting that things that are wrong in the world do not have to be this way, by choosing to live courageously and joyfully, by creating beauty, by doing good. As Paul would urge followers of Jesus living in the capital of the Roman empire: "Don't let evil conquer you, but conquer evil by doing good" (Romans 12:21).

Because we believe there is more, hope inspires and allows us to risk ourselves—and the ultimate such risk is to love: "people who truly hope as the resurrection encourages us to hope will be people enabled to love in a new way. Conversely, people who are living

"And his name will be the hope of all the world."

by this rule of love will be people who are learning more deeply how to hope."[1] This changes every relationship, every interaction and every attitude. In the pattern of the stories of the birth of Jesus, this means profound humility and costly generosity, with good news for all people but a particular concern for the lowly.

The first followers of Jesus understood that their—and our—invitations to be agents of resistance and hope somehow play a role in enacting the realities of the kingdom of God in our world: "Our great desire is that you will keep on loving others as long as life lasts, in order to make certain that what you hope for will come true" (Hebrews 6:11). While we might consider ourselves insignificant, that whatever we do does not really matter, the Bible writers insisted that our choices, decisions and priorities matter, even as some kind of voice or vote for how the world ought to be.

And our pre-eminent choice is how we respond to Jesus. It might be the murderous rage of Herod or the indifference of the Jewish religious leaders. It might be the initial fear but growing acceptance of Zechariah and Joseph. It might be the wonder and praise of Elizabeth and Mary. It might be the joy of the shepherds and the magi. It might be the satisfied expectation of Simeon and Anna. It might be the hope of a world transformed, a life renewed and a restoration promised.

For those closest to Jesus—the first people who told and re-told the stories of His birth, life, death and resurrection—His story changed everything. His kingdom was the new reality and a new future for them and for our world. Hope happened—and hope happens still.

In Jesus, something happened.

In Jesus' birth, something happened that was so significant that every year we pause and sing songs about it, share gifts with each other and re-tell the story.

Jesus happened—"and his name will be the hope of all the world" (Matthew 12:21).

1. N T Wright, *Surprised by Hope: Rethinking Heaven, the Resurrection, and the Mission of the Church*, HarperOne, 2008, page 288.

All who heard the shepherds' story were astonished, but Mary kept all these things in her heart and thought about them often.

—Luke 2:18, 19

Thanks

This book is dedicated to Angela, to whom I have now been married for more than half of my life. Over that time, she has endured my complicated relationship with Christmas, including my sometimes cynical and curmudgeonly attitudes, as well as sporadic sentimentality towards selected Christmas music and my fascination with the story itself. She justifiably laughed at my project of writing a Christmas book but was the first reader of each chapter as I was writing. Thank you for your many contributions to my projects and to me. Thank you for being married to me for so long and let's continue to try to live in ways that are shaped by the biggest and best stories but that also make space for the smallest and forgotten.

Thanks to those who read this book as a manuscript—including Bruce Manners, Peter Roennfeldt, Joanna Darby, Joshua Stothers, Tony Knight, Lyndelle Peterson and Kevin Geelan—for their feedback, suggestions, encouragement and endorsements.

Thanks to Tim Costello for his support of this project by his generous endorsement. I have been a long-time admirer of his work as an Australian Christian leader, so I am honoured to have him read and contribute to this project in this way.

Thanks to David Edgren for his permission to share the story behind his story in Chapter 9. His stories are worth checking out.

Thanks to the management of Signs Publishing and the publishing committee that supported the writing and distribution of this book. Thanks to Andrew Irvine for his personal support and encouragement, as well as the work that he does in leading the Signs team. Thanks to Lauren Webb for joining our editorial team this year and doing the editorial work on this project. Thanks also to the production team at Signs that made it a book.

Thanks to the Road to Bethlehem team in Melbourne and the great thing they have done over more than 25 years to faithfully and creatively re-tell the story of the birth of Jesus. It has been a privilege to be a small part of this team over the past few years and to see the passion and good work of so many people in this setting, at the same time as being uniquely immersed in the story.

And "thank God for this gift too wonderful for words!" (2 Corinthians 9:15).

Further Invitation

We invite you to discover more about the story of Jesus and why it matters, how it can change your life and the difference it can make in our world. It is so much more than a story to tell only in the season of Christmas.

To sign up for an online course to learn more about Jesus and His story or to find more books like this one, use the QR code or visit:

www.signspublishing.com.au/Advent

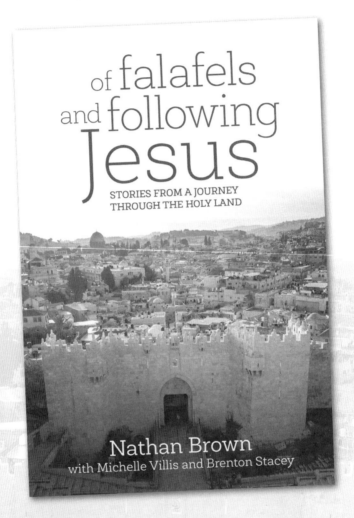

Nathan Brown is a writer and book editor, based near Melbourne, Australia. He holds degrees in law, literature, English, writing, and theology and justice. Nathan is author or editor of 16 previous books, including *Of Falafels and Following Jesus*, *For the Least of These*, *Why I Try to Believe*, *Do Justice* and *Nemesis Train* (a novel). He continues to write regularly for publications around the world. Find other books by Nathan at

www.amazon.com/Nathan-Brown/e/B001JSB9EI

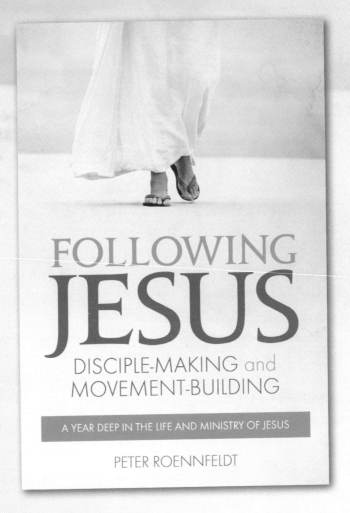